BOLIVIA HILL
BIRTH MOTHER

PIET VALLEI

Ordering Information:

Prime Seven Media
518 Landmann St.
Tomah City, WI 54660

Printed in the United States of America

Table of Contents

Introduction

This is part two of *The Bolivia Hill Foundling*. It is about the foundling's birth mother and how the baby came to be abandoned at Bolivia Hill.

In part one references were made to Andrew Tate, a controversial influencer of young men and boys in the so-called incel culture of young males who are frustrated with their lack of success in relationships with females. Among Tate's male supremacist views, he advocated choking and rape of girls and women. (https://en.wikipedia.org/wiki/Andrew_Tate) Near the end of part one, an adult Tate follower trapped 6-year-old Eppie. He choked and raped her using Tate's methods.

A common definition of 'Rape' may be found in the Queensland *Criminal Code Act* at section 349 (a), (b) and (c). It tells us rape is more than penile penetration without consent. It may also involve penetration of any bodily orifice with a finger or a tongue, as well as non-human implements like a knife, a stick, a pen, or a dildo. A child under 16 legally cannot consent.

The toxic young men in this second part of *The Bolivia Hill Foundling* pre-date Tate's influencing and methods he advocated but are part of the same incel culture which he focusses on. Their rape activities through their 'Three Musketeers' club mask their own senses of inadequacy. Yet, as we will see with examples cited of pack rapes in the Queensland town of Ingham during the 1970s, in California with the 'Spur Posse' group in 1993, and the cricket players' sexual conquest game in England during 2019, toxic masculinity among young men and boys is not new.

In 2005 a 10-year-old girl in foster care with the Queensland Department of Child Safety was gang raped by nine men and boys repeatedly during several days in the town of Aurukun. She was a foetal alcohol syndrome victim who the judge said "probably agreed" to repeated sex with them. (How can any 10-year-old child legally agree to sex let alone agree to repeated gang rapes?) This was a major headline scandal in Australia for several weeks. The maximum penalty for the oldest was only six years in jail. The young boys and men (aged from under 10 to 27) targeted her simply because she was a little girl who was available, easy to dupe, and easy to satisfy their unrequited toxic masculinity. Moreover, she contracted gonorrhoea from the encounters and threatened suicide. She had also previously been gang raped by juveniles in 2002. (https://web.archive.org/web/ 20071212163927/http:// www.theaustralian.news.com.au/story/0,25197,22902781-601,00.html)

Over the years there have been so many examples of little girls raped by young boys and older men driven to violate. A Google search will find a constant flow of cases in Australia, the USA, Britain, Portugal, India, Germany, South Africa, and elsewhere. It is common. But, often perpetrators, victims, and communities are protected from publicity by law.

In this second part, brief reference is made to a case in 2023 when an 11-year-old boy in foster care in Queensland on two separate occasions strangled and sexually abused a foster care girl. (*Courier Mail, Brisbane,* 12 July 2023, page 3.) He did this Tate style. Children in foster care are especially vulnerable. But, with privacy provisions within child protection laws in every state in Australia (such as the Queensland *Child Protection Act* at section 189) very little publicity occurs when children 'in care' are abused. A rare example of where publicity and resulting widespread public anger about a vulnerable foster care child did occur despite the secrecy provisions of the law was the case of 12-year-old Queensland foster care girl Tiahleigh Palmer. She was raped several times and then murdered. (https://en.wikipedia.org/wiki/ Murder_of_Tiahleigh_Palmer)

In March 2025 a group of little boys raped a 5-year-old girl at their school in Sydney. Because of what those little 5-year-old boys did to her, she had to have hospital treatment for her internal injuries. A few days later at the same Sydney school another 5-year-old girl complained about a similar assault but by a different little boy. (https://www.facebook.com/2GBSydney/photos/exclusive-another-5-year-old-girl-has-reported-been-sexually-assaulted-at-sydney/1167475205390184/)

The very young ages of some of the perpetrators in these cases raises a fundamental issue: is toxic masculinity deeply embedded in our society's psyche? And, no matter how many prison terms are meted out to perpetrators and no matter how many education programs are provided, will toxic masculinity ever be eradicated? In part one, we saw that the man who found newborn Eppie at Bolivia Hill went to great lengths to protect her as she grew.

This part two of *The Bolivia Hill Foundling* story is about the tragic outcome of toxic masculinity for an intelligent and sensitive 17-year-old girl during her first year at university. She was well above the age of consent but certainly did not consent when she was drugged unconscious. Apart from developing a hatred of men, the repercussions of that gang rape were for her just terrible. Eppie, the newborn baby girl who an elderly man found abandoned at Bolivia Hill, was the product of that gang rape. As will be seen in the last five lines at the end of this second part, she likely inherited her birth mother's misandry. Yet conversely, growing 6-year-old Eppie's own experiences of toxic masculinity reinforced her adoration of that elderly man.

So, dear reader, please read on.

Some Notes

Note 1: This part of the story should be read within the context of what has been happening at Australian universities recently. It was written with the following report in mind:

> Heywood, W., Myers, P., Powell, A., Meikle, G., & Nguyen, D. (2022). *National Student Safety Survey: Report on the prevalence of sexual harassment and sexual assault among university students in 2021.* Melbourne: The Social Research Centre. https://universitiesaustralia.edu.au/wp-content/uploads/2022/03/2021-NSSS-National-Report.pdf

Note 2: The author worked in a student support and advisory capacity at an Australian university for twenty years and also taught at a teachers college in Nigeria as well as at a high school in Australia and two high schools in Zambia.

Note 3: The main characters are fictitious.

Note 4: Internet references cited were functional at date of publication, although some have a 'paywall' and require a subscription or free membership for access.

Note 5: Photographs without acknowledgement were taken by the author. The main front cover photo is by the author. The inset photo is by *Depositphotos* and posed by a model who is used as a model in many other photos in this part of the story.

Note 6: The age of consent is 16 years in Australian states and in New Zealand, Britain, and South Africa. In European Union countries it varies between 14 and 17. But, as in other societies, in this story there is an under current of misogyny among young men. They tend to see girls and young women like Cathy as legitimate targets because it is a male prerogative to focus their sexual desires on young girls by any means available.

Note 7: In this story Cathy has a terrible experience on her 17th birthday and it likely has a profound effect on the child she has conceived and after the birth.[1]

Note 8: Some university students in this story are studying towards degrees. Three are doing a Bachelor of Commerce (BCom) which takes three years. Others are studying for a Law degree (LLB) which takes four years. The heroine of the story is doing a three year Bachelor of Creative Arts.

---

[1] See: Sapolsky, R. (2023), *Determined: Life without Free Will.* The Bodley Head (Penguin), London.

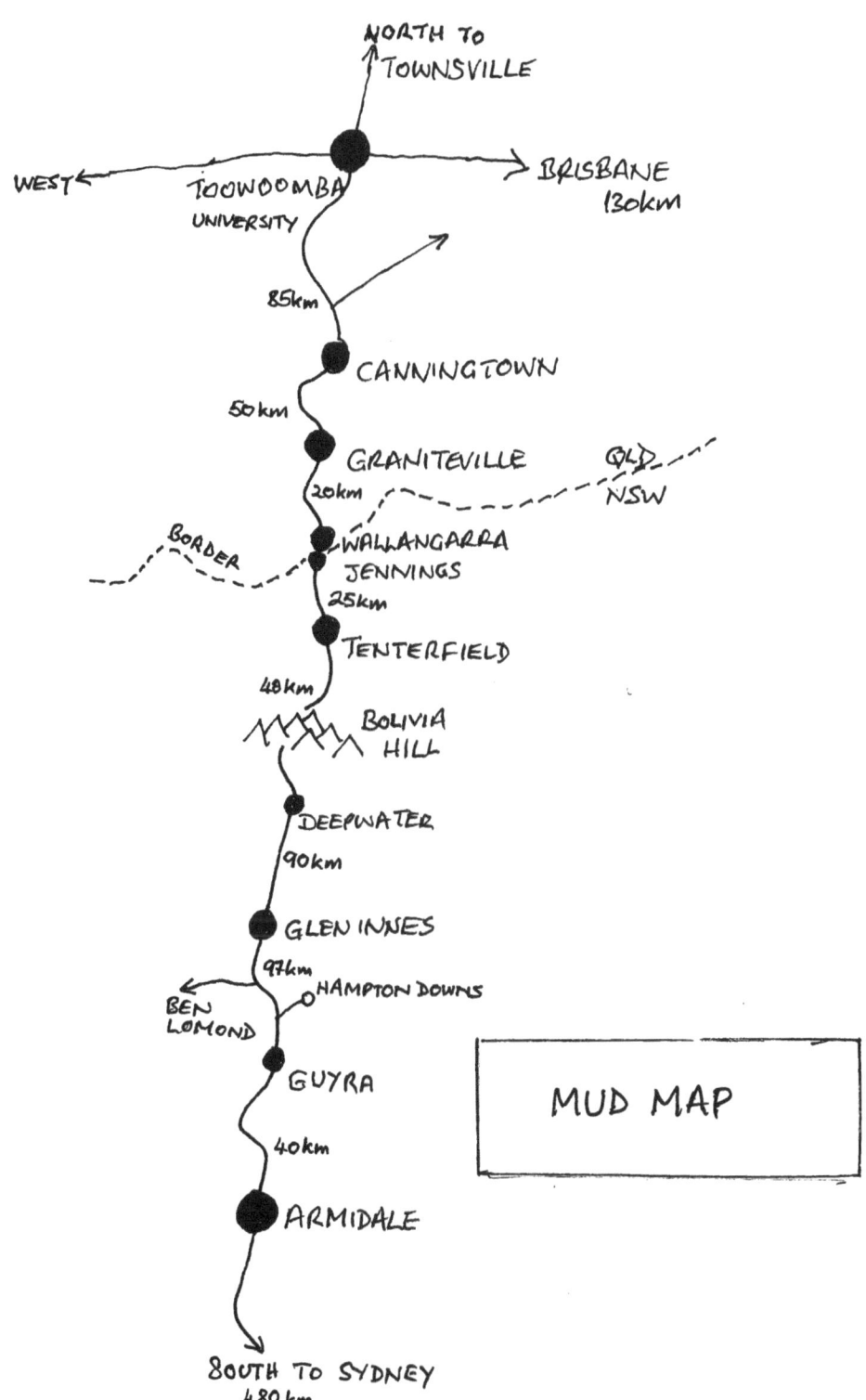

Cathy is a first year student at the University in Toowoomba. She grew up on the family's sheep grazing property, Hampton Downs, north-east of Guyra in New South Wales.

The Squatter Girl

Catherine Morton is a 'fresher' University student from country northern New South Wales. She is still 16 turning 17 in March. She is starting a full-time Bachelor of Creative Arts course at the Toowoomba University in Queensland. A pretty, small statured girl with long light brown hair which she wears in plaits, she invariably dresses in very prim and proper clothes and never wears make-up. She is fit and supple. Her skin is clear and blemish-free, a 'peaches and cream' complexion. Because she is relatively small, almost flat-chested and slim at only 157cm high, she looks very young almost like a 13-year-old girl.

(*Depositpotos*. Posed by model)

Cathy, as her family call her (except when her Mother is angry, which is often, and she becomes "Cather-ine!"), comes from a pastoral property in northern New South Wales around 20km north of the town of Guyra in high country at 1,200 metres above sea level. It snows most winters. Called "Hampton Downs", it has always grazed sheep, usually Merinos. But, they have recently diversified into black-faced Dorpers. Mr and Mrs Morton are now in their seventies and Cathy is the last of the line. They hope that she will someday take over and run the family property.

The undulating granite country of their property near Tubbamurra northeast of Guyra in summer and winter. The entry to the family's 520 hectare property is two kilometres east of the New England Highway. Also seen here during winter.

Some of the property's Merino wool sheep and some of the Dorper sheep which are for meat. (*Right*) Shearing under way in the farm's shearing shed.

Her family has owned and operated their property, Hampton Downs, since the 1830s. They are descendants of the original 'squatters' from England who claimed, settled and farmed the 'run'. The original property was about 2,000ha but it has been subdivided a number of times. The Morton family live in the homestead which is a relatively small but rather grand 100-year-old building. The property is well-run but at only 520ha now, it has become almost too small to be viable. They try to maintain standards but sometimes live beyond their means and this is reflected in the way Cathy is parented with no expense spared. They graze sheep as was the case 100 years ago but no longer exclusively Merinos. So, there is a shearing shed. Shearers descend on the property every year after the cold winter months and the wool goes mainly to China these days. They also have Dorper sheep for mutton.

Although the homestead is over 100 years old, it is not the original one. A relatively small homestead, it is still quite grand. Cathy's mother takes great care of it, especially the beautiful interior rooms. The garden is also well looked after. The homestead is her pride and joy. Cathy is banned from the main living room except on special occasions. The family employs a full-time stockman, his wife to work in the house, a part-time gardener, and a governess for Cathy until she is eleven. The payroll for the property is a significant drain on finances.

(*Left*) The shearers' quarters. (*Right*) This is the full-time stockman's house seen during winter.

As an only child, Cathy has lived an isolated life on the family property. She has been taught proper manners from the time she could first walk, like greeting adults correctly, standing up straight, sitting up straight at meals, holding her knife and fork the correct way, never putting her elbows on the table, putting cutlery straight when she has finished, and never leaving the table without asking permission and so on. Her clothes are demure and understated for a girl. She has to make her bed every morning and her mother checks that she has done it correctly. She is not allowed to shout or make rude gestures. As an old squatter family they have standards to maintain.

(*Left*) The Morton's well-cared for but modest homestead. (*Right*) The Benson's homestead is run down. It is no longer lived in and is used as a storage shed.

Their homestead is really quite modest compared to some but her mother is a bit of a social climber and this is part of her motivation "to maintain standards". She often reminds Cathy about the Bensons living on a nearby property: "They are not squatters and have let their homestead and the whole squatter way of life go to ruins."

She has always known of her family's squatter heritage which has been instilled in her almost from birth. So, she tends to see herself and her family as different from others, almost superior. During sheep shearing her mother has been known to keep her away from the shearers and occupy her with other things. "You don't want to mix with riff-raff like that." Her mother is also aware of the old tradition that it is an ill omen for women and girls to be in a shearing shed when shearing is in full swing.

 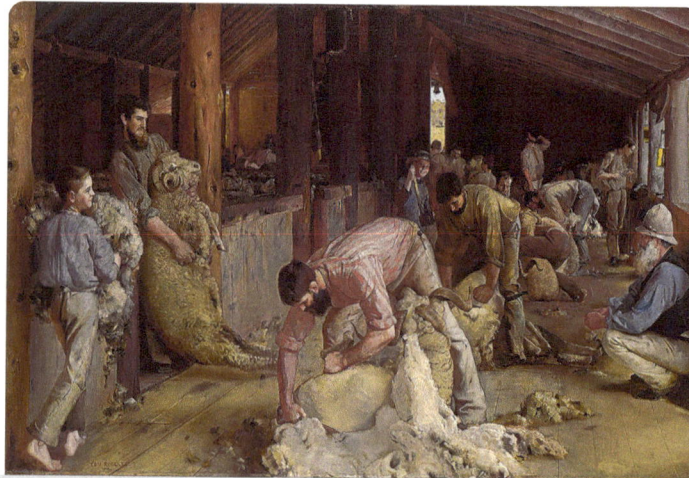

Tom Roberts: *Shearing the Rams* 1890. (*Public domain*) Cathy loves this classic Australian impressionist painting. She very is familiar with the annual shearing on Hampton Downs.

Shearing the Rams by Tom Roberts was painted in 1890 near Corowa on the NSW/Victoria border, showing a busy shearing shed. But, Tom Roberts put a deliberate 'error' into the painting. He shows a little nine-year-old girl, Susan Bourne, in the middle background of the picture and working as the 'tar boy' (who would put tar on accidental sheep wounds caused by shears). Until fairly recently, it was unheard of for a female to be present during shearing. So, Cathy's mother is particularly annoyed when she hears that young Cathy recently helped a 'roustabout'[2] with general sweeping during shearing.

(Depositphotos. Posed by models)

---

[2] "Roustabout" in *Wikipedia* at https://en.wikipedia.org/wiki/Roustabout_A roustabout is shearing shed worker with broad-based, non-specific skills like floor sweeping and bringing tar to the shearers when called upon.

She gives eleven-year-old Cathy a roasting: "I told you! Don't go to the shearing shed! … Now, go to your room and put your plaits back. You're older now and with your hair down like this you look cheap! Also, change out of those jeans. Put on a respectable dress!" Obediently, Cathy says: "Yes, Mother." She does what she is told. (At her mother's insistence, it is always "Mother", not low class "Mum" or "Mummy".)

The well-maintained Hampton Downs homestead is over 100 years old with lovely gracious period heritage rooms.

As committed Anglicans, the family goes to St James Anglican Church in Guyra on most Sundays and sit at the same pew every time. In fact, that pew is usually left vacant for them even if they don't turn up. It has always been the Morton family's pew, virtually for a century. Later, while she is at boarding school, during the holidays she takes a small Sunday school class at Guyra. The little kids look up to her admiringly as a rôle model. The elderly ladies of the parish love her.

A regime of strict training in show jumping and dressage at an early age. (*iStockphotos*. Posed by models)

Cathy is good with horses and handling livestock. Between the ages of about eight and eleven she did quite a bit of show jumping, regularly attending pony club meets and competing at country town shows across northern New South Wales and even into Queensland. This involved a lot of laborious practice jumping at home but usually she had to be cajoled into practicing. Her mother was strict and demanding in teaching her to ride, then to show jump, and then do dressage.

She even learned to ride side-saddle. Her Mother told her: "This is the proper ladylike way to ride. And, the Queen does." Her Father would trailer her pony in a horse float long distances to pony club meets and agricultural shows on some weekends. However, this is what they wanted for her, not necessarily what she wanted for herself.

She professes to like country and western music and her favourite would seem to be Slim Dusty. Yet, this liking is part of her subtle reaction to family pressure on her to conform to being seen as a 'country girl'. So, life for her on this property was not a bed of roses. Her relationship with both parents was more often than not cold and distant. Both her parents were quite strict and authoritarian but always wanted what they believed was the best for their daughter, especially in terms her manners, culture and skills. Simple things like the correct way to hold a knife and fork, how to eat soup, etc. were drummed into her. Almost invariably she complied and conformed. Until she went away to boarding school she was closer to the governess than to her parents.

From the age of five she has had piano lessons and so reads music. An elderly lady from a neighbouring property would drive over once or twice a week to teach her. After each lesson, her time on the piano with long practice sessions was always alone. She loved that time alone and the privacy of the practice sessions

(iStockphoto. Posed by model)

even though her mother would be elsewhere in the house listening to make sure she practiced properly. She would daydream as she practiced. So, she now actually loves classical music more than country and western, especially that of the baroque, classical, and romantic periods: Bach, Mozart and Beethoven. That is why she has chosen to do Music as a major in her University degree.

She would also spend much time alone on the verandah reading. Her parents considered this as good; she was being 'ladylike'. She also had an increasing interest in art, particularly art of the nineteenth and twentieth centuries. She loved Tom Roberts paintings and those by Namatjira which are very Australian. But her tastes also included paintings by artists as diverse as Turner and Klimt.

Thus, she is a cultured lass and this was her parents' intention. It is expected that because of this subtly groomed and austere upbringing, she will grow up to be a very eligible wife with another well-endowed old established family or more hopefully at this property. But, the other side to this upbringing is that she was pressured into these activities. Like her show jumping, she was pushed by her parents who wanted the best for her. She preferred riding horses alone for stock control on the property. Piano practice sessions were also often quite coerced affairs, especially by her mother who was rather old fashioned, domineering and sometimes shouted commands. So, Cathy was definitely a loner, usually preferring her own company. Yet, she was never rebellious, just about always co-operative and compliant. That was her nature. She was born that way. So, she was a model teenager. She got on relatively well with her father and liked his company. They sometimes had fun together when they were out riding. But, she was never really close to him, emotionally. There was always a slight distance between them, probably because her domineering mother would encourage her to be more ladylike all the time. And, because of that, he also expected it of Cathy. In fact, Cathy was never close to anyone, almost an archetypal loner.

Shortly after her birth, her parents bought Cathy some shares in Medibank Private for her to inherit at age seventeen. A sound investment as during the last nearly seventeen years, they have grown in value in leaps and bounds especially as interest payments are re-invested.

Now starting at University in Toowoomba, she has never had a boyfriend. She is too much of an introspective loner. And, her parents, especially her mother, have always chaperoned her in an old fashioned way when out socially. She has never reacted badly to this, seemingly to accept it as normal; an attitude probably brought about by her isolation on the family property. She has had strong family values instilled in her from birth. The 'family' is most important to her parents and now to her. Thus, she has been groomed to have a strong bond to her family heritage and to it as a support in her life. In the occasional play times with her father, she would always have to take a traditional, but not necessarily submissive, female or ladylike rôle. That is because women in the family have traditionally been seen as the stable foundation of their family: the *materfamilias* in Latin. It is expected that one day Cathy will fill that kind of rôle. Sons and husbands can be errant but not daughters and wives. The family depends on them being rock solid. That is why she is doing a three-year Bachelor of Creative Arts degree, nothing so specialised and career-oriented as Education, Law, or Psychology. This generalist degree would fit in with her future rôle as a *materfamilias* on a rural property. Later, if she needed specialist qualifications, she could always do a graduate diploma. And, she has chosen to do Music as her main subject area in her undergraduate degree.

As per her mother's wishes, Cathy never really got involved in boy-type rough and tumble games with her father. Nevertheless, with her riding and life on the property she is slim and fit.

This family has lived on the property since squatter days and she knows the history of the area well. She has strong feelings about the dreadful 1838 Myall Creek Massacre which was on a property not much more than 150 kilometres away.[3] She has been to the simple but very moving memorial which overlooks the grand Myall Creek Station homestead in the valley below. But, she doesn't actually feel guilt about what was done. After all, it was not the squatter land owners who did it but the farm hands and stockmen who her mother would call "riff raff" or "scrapings from London prisons", the convicts who the transportation ships brought to Australia. (Typically, she ignores that a neighbouring squatter lead the gang.) Nevertheless, even though it happened a very long time ago, early in the nineteenth century, she does feel modern white society should in some ways atone for what was done.

(*Left*) The big, grand, and very impressive "Myall Creek Station" homestead. By comparison, the Morton's "Hampton Downs" homestead is modest. (*Right*) One of several memorial plaques on the hill overlooking the Myall Creek valley.

---

[3] See: "Myall Creek Massacre" in *Wikipedia* at https://en.wikipedia.org/wiki/Myall_Creek_massacre

As a ten-year-old, she has read Doris Garimara's *Rabbit Proof Fence* [4] and was engrossed in what happened to the two little girls. She felt an affinity with them. She was also deeply moved about the story, not only because of the racial oppression involved but by the notion of removing children from their families. She thinks foster care is wrong. She would hate to be removed from her family. Later, at boarding school she learns about the "Stolen Generations".[5] Her upset about removal of children from their families is very strong because, for her, family is so important. So, there is a sense of moral concern in her. Some of this comes from her High Church Anglican Church background which has been instilled in her from an early age. She sees her Christianity as a guiding light for life, kindness, and social justice and with Jesus as the shining example.

With this squatter background, some call it a 'squattocracy'[6] heritage, she has a squattocracy speech pattern and accent.[7] She never uses words such as 'like', 'kinda', 'ginna', and 'ya know' repeatedly scattered throughout her speech which is the fashion today. She never uses modern young peoples' adjectives like 'cool', 'sick' and 'awesome'. She never greets anyone with the American 'Hi', always saying a proper 'Good morning' or 'Good afternoon' etc. She doesn't even use the Australian 'G'day' as her mother says this is for farm hands and stockmen.

Until the age of eleven, she was taught at home by a governess, a mature woman in her mid- fifties. This is their long-standing family tradition. Then, when the governess retired, her parents sent her to the public K-12 Guyra Central School for a

---

[4] Pilkington Garimara, D., *Rabbit Proof Fence*, University of Queensland Press, Brisbane 1981.

[5] See "Stolen Generations" in *Wikipedia* at https://en.wikipedia.org/wiki/Stolen_Generations
     See especially: Lavarch, M. (1997), *Bringing Them Home: Report of the National Inquiry into Separation of Aboriginal and Torres Strait Islander Children from Their Families*, Canberra: Commonwealth of Australia, Human Rights and Equal Opportunities Commission. https://www.humanrights.gov.au/our-work/bringing-them-home-report-1997

[6] For background to the "squattocracy", see *Wikipedia* at https://en.wikipedia.org/wiki/Squatting_(Australia)

[7] For a typical example of a 'squattocracy' speech pattern and accent, listen to Tamie Fraser who is the widow of former Prime Minister, Malcolm Fraser. https://www.youtube.com/watch?v=TEiWbTosWEc .At this 'Don Lane Show', scroll ahead 29 minutes to hear Tamie Fraser talking. This is how Cathy speaks: see how Tamie says "private life". Her parents on both sides had a long history in the pastoral industry dating back tot he 1840s. She grew up on her parents' sheep property in Victoria and spent her early years being taught by a governess before being sent to boarding school at the age of nine. Her husband, Malcolm Fraser had a similar wealthy 'squattocracy' background on a large sheep property in Victoria, was also taught by a governess until the age of ten when he was sent to boarding school.

year in Year 7. This turned out to be a failure. She was teased because of her accent and accused of being snooty. It was a form of class warfare. Sometimes, the teasing was outright bullying and a bit violent because she would stand up for herself. On the school bus she used to sit up front right behind the driver for protection. Kids liked pulling her plaits. Thus, she tended to shy away from team sports but her three saving graces were that she was very pretty, academically advanced, and was good at athletics. It was a very unhappy one year at primary school.

So, from the start of Year 8 just before she turned 12, her parents sent her away to boarding school in Queensland. She was enrolled at the Anglican St Agnes boarding school on the Gold Coast where she had no such speech pattern bullying issues. There were many other girls like her as most of the boarders were from

St Agnes School on the Gold Coast.

pastoral properties out west. She was much happier there. But, one reason her mother sent her there was to ensure she didn't do things like going to the shearing shed during shearing or mix with jackaroos who would come to work on the property seasonally.

Cathy was at St Agnes until she finished Year 12 four months before she turned 17. Indeed, these were happy years for her, even though she was always quiet and reclusive, shunned team sports and preferred her own company. At the school she pretended to be a Country and Western fan, especially for Slim Dusty. And, she pretended to like current singers like Dami Im, Taylor Swift, Lady Gaga, and even Justin Bieber. But, again she really preferred Bach, Handel and Beethoven and loved her piano practice times alone. Nevertheless, she even used to look forward to returning to school after the holidays. At St Agnes she also learned about computers and use of the internet. She loved *Wikipedia* because it was so useful for her academic studies. And, she maintained e-mail and *Skype* contact with family at home. However, she never accessed *Facebook* or *Instagram*. These were not only beneath her but with her experience of being bullied at Guyra Public School and more recently aware of Dolly Everett's suicide at a boarding school in Warwick,[8] she is resolute in having nothing to do with internet social media.

Boarding at St Agnes, she couldn't be in the show jumping circuit, something she rather liked not to have to do, but she continues her piano lessons. She takes up Gymnastics which she finds she loves. She is not only good at it but very enthusiastic. It is a very individual focussed sport and through her Gymnastics she loves being fit and trim.

During this time, she has access to a good school library and the internet. She develops an interest in art, mainly because that is one of her academic subjects. The internet is wonderful for not only finding information about past painters like Bruegel, van Gogh, Rembrandt, Goya, and those of the Italian Renaissance but also for viewing works of art. She is especially interested because artworks by famous past artists reflect so much of history and social values. She likes more recent Australian impressionist painters like Arthur Streeton, Frederick McCubbin, and Tom Roberts because they beautifully show Australia the way it was. At a young age she already knew about Tom Roberts' *Shearing of the Rams* and now sees so much more in terms of society in the painting. Yet, while a prude she also likes Norman Lindsay's naked women. She feels he is venerating women as sensual beings who show a natural sexuality that she has had to suppress in her past.

At St Agnes she was aware that some boarding girls used to sneak out on Friday or Saturday nights, climbing the fence and making their way to the night life at Surfers Paradise before sneaking back before dawn. The rather straight-laced Cathy would have nothing to do with this and saw it as morally quite wrong. She believed the boarders who did this were not real country girls but more than likely girls from 'broken' urban families, something which was not true. Some of those adventurous girls were from outback pastoral properties. Indeed, some had even been sent to

---

[8] O'Brien, K., "Cyber-bullying campaign launched after suicide of Akubra face Amy 'Dolly' Everett", *ABC News*, Sydney, 10 January 2018. https://www.abc.net.au/news/2018-01-10/dolly-everett-nt-suicide-cyber-bullying-campaign- launched/9317056 Also: "Suicide of Dolly Everett" in *Wikipedia* at https://en.wikipedia.org/wiki/ Suicide_of_Dolly_Everett Dolly was bullied by school mates at Scotts College in Warwick where she was boarder. It got so bad that during one school holidays she shot herself. She lived with her family in the Northern Territory.

boarding school precisely to remove their developing and precocious daughters from contact with young Jackaroos. Yet, their parents back at home had no idea what they got up to at school on weekend nights. Nor did the school.[9] During her Year 12 at St Agnes, she ended up being made a prefect. But, she was a strict prefect, formal and not very popular.

---

[9]   The author once taught for several years at a girls' boarding school on the Gold Coast and knew about this.

CHAPTER 2

Cathy as a fresher

C athy started University about a month before her 17th birthday. Most, but not all 'fresher' students, are already 18. In the the mid-year semester break she passed her driving test and got her P1 (Provisional) NSW driver's licence. So, it became possible for her to drive between the farm and Toowoomba. It is up to five hours by road between Toowoomba and Guyra. During the first part of the year, her parents drive her to and from University. So, for the start of this her first year at University, she travels to Toowoomba with her mother in the family's Toyota Prado, arriving two days before the start of OrientationWeek. Her mother returns to the farm two days later.

Her mother helped settle her in at one of the University's three on-campus residential colleges. She has a room with a shared toilet/bathroom. She also has 21 meals a week. So, she is well catered for. She and her mother are very happy about the new tertiary education life just about to begin for her. She is excited but understandably also nervous. Mother is particularly concerned. She tends to hover around, making sure Cathy's room is set up and organised properly. She warns her about intruders: "Young bucks will want to come into your room. They'll make excuses like helping with assignments. Keep your room as your own private space, my dear. And, always lock your door, not just when you go out but when you are in this cosy little room. You just never know. Look after your key, too."

"Yes, Mother." Cathy is getting a little bored with her Mother's 'helicoptering'. She wants her life to be as she wants it.

After her mother has left, she nevertheless does take her Mother's advice. She has never really been on her own. Boarding school at St Agnes wasn't on her own. It was very organised. Now, she really is alone and a little worried. She is very shy when she meets fellow 'freshers', not realising they are also shy and nervous. She dutifully attends all the 'O-Week' orientation and enrolment procedures and activities. She is keen to find out. It really is the start of a new and exciting life for her. She has lived a sheltered, cosseted and chaperoned isolated life both at home and at boarding school. This has left her ill-equipped to deal with the cut and thrust of the realities of University social life especially among young people. Realising this, she tends to be timid, reserved, and reclusive, avoiding social activities more so than others. During 'O-Week', she especially avoids the parties and social events organised by the Resident Student Club. She fears them as drinking orgies. Like a scared and worried new dog, she tends to be reclusive, shunning social interaction even with other 'freshers' like her and spending much of the Orientation Week and the first teaching week in her room, the library or out jogging by herself. This becomes the pattern of her first year existence at University: a shy reclusive student. Yet, she is attractive and need not be so reticent.

As already mentioned, Cathy is a pretty, fine featured, small statured girl with below shoulder length light brown hair in plaits and she is fit and supple. Her skin is clear and blemish- free, a 'peaches and cream' complexion. Because she is relatively small and slim at only 157cm high, she looks very young almost like a little girl. And, her demure understated clothes seem to promote this. She wears glasses most of the time. She never wears make-up or nail varnish and her clothes are always modest dresses, more proper for a young girl of her family's perceived status and background. She never wears very short shorts or low cut tops. In her family's and in her terms, these clothes are too revealing and not 'ladylike'. Thus, tight-fitting or revealing and sexy clothes are a definite no-no for her. When she is out jogging by herself, she wears a T-shirt and quite long denim shorts. And, she would never dream of having a tattoo or any form of piercing, not even for ear rings.

Yet, during one of her first lectures in a large lecture theatre she has no idea that others find her attractive. A pair of young male 'freshers' have a short whispered conversation.

One says: "See that girl there. That one by herself with glasses. Wow! I'd sure like to get to know her."

His friend says: "Hey! Keep your mind on Educational Philosophy! … Yeah, I seen her. I've noticed her. I fancy her, too. Like, I wish she was mine."

After the lecture, they look for her but she has quickly taken herself off to the library.

Cathy is so very naïve. Most students her age are not as unworldly as she is. She does have an iPhone but has no *Facebook*, *Instagram*, *Twitter* or *Snapchat* accounts. Every teenager of her age has at least one and has had one since primary school days. Not Cathy. Her conservative family eschewed and condemned them. She continues going to Church on Sundays while in Toowoomba. She walks to the St Matthew's Anglican Church at Drayton about two kilometres away. She also continues to never wear make-up. At University, she is shy and private, keeping to herself. It is as if the outside real world is now too scary for her. Landed alone at a regional University in a country city really has been a shock for her. Brisbane or Sydney would have been terrifying. She just could not have handled being thrown into University life there.

As a result and reminiscent of her unfortunate Guyra Central School days, during the first three weeks she has quickly developed a little bit of a reputation at University for being aloof, snooty, and frigid. Seeing this pretty and always well-dressed very young looking girl in very modest demure clothes, some older 'returner' male students snigger among themselves about what they would like to do to her: grab her and show her the way. And, 'returner' girls roll their eyes and look the other way while commenting: "Where did she come from?" (However, as we shall see, after Cathy's first three weeks, her shyness and reluctance to mix suddenly become extreme.)

During these first weeks, she sometimes sees young lovers kissing and getting really involved with each other. Not used to this, she looks away in embarrassment and continues walking to her lecture or tutorial. As a farm girl with cattle, sheep, and dogs on the property, she tends to see this as almost like humans mating in public.

(iStockphoto. Posed by models.)

Yet, Cathy is not unlike quite a few other students at University. Not all students are wild drinkers and party goers. Many female and male students remain virgins during their time at University and do so out of choice. There are Baptist, Salvation Army, Quaker, devout Catholics and even just home-schooled youths. Like her, they dress modestly and tend to stay away from partying activities. She is probably more like the home-schooled types for she is not fervently religious although she is a committed conservative or High Church Anglican and went to an Anglican boarding school. This conservatism is something which has added to her being cautious and shy about social gatherings.

Young late teenage students are very hasty to make judgements about each other and to sum up others. This is especially so in group situations like at University. *Twitter* and *Snapchat* accounts can run hot. Gossip can escalate rapidly. And, because of their age, sex is also a prevalent undercurrent in that gossip. By the end of the first couple of weeks, she is known for being cold towards other students and speculation among both 'fresher' and 'returner' male and female students is that she is a virgin, which is true.[10] And, of course, she is not on the pill or any other form of contraception. "I'm just not that sort". She knows about the pill and condoms but has never actually seen them or been interested. In her old-fashioned conservative way, she presumes she should reserve herself for her life with a future husband.

Thus, a small group of young predatory-minded male third year Commerce students have been around the campus assessing this year's crop of 'fresher' girls. They call themselves the 'Three Musketers': Errol, Flash, and Hugh, all nicknames not their real names. For example, 'Hugh' is the name his three mates gave him, after they likened him to British film actor Hugh Grant, his sexual exploits and his infamy for being arrested for committing a 'lewd act' in the USA.[11] They find that very American word 'lewd' quite funny. They also think of former *Playboy* magazine owner Hugh Hefner who had so many beautiful girls over so many years.[12] Errol is named after Australian film star of the 1950s Errol Flynn who was famous for

---

[10] Only 46% of 17-year-olds have had sex. (2019), *National Survey of Australian Secondary Students*, La Trobe University, Melbourne. http://www.teenhealth.org.au So, as a 17-year-old, conservative Cathy is not alone. She is actually in a small majority.

[11] Rodrigues, J. "Hugh Grant arrested with sex worker 20 years ago." *The Guardian*, London, 26 June 2015. https://www.theguardian.com/film/from-the-archive-blog/2015/jun/26/hugh-grant-arrest-prostitute-divine-brown-20-1995

[12] See *Wikipedia* at https://en.wikipedia.org/wiki/Hugh_Hefner

having so many girls he had no time for foreplay. Hence the phrase: "In like Flynn." Many were alleged to be under age. Flash was named after mythical American comic character Flash Gordon.

This small group are not just earthy and risqué in their discussions but they share quite vulgar and very indecent jokes among themselves about girls they see as needing to be shown the way: "I'd like to get up her", "I fancy the taste of her pussy", and "I wanna take out her hymen!" Then, there's that old rhyme: "When roses are red, they're red for plucking. When girls are sixteen, they're ready for …" These are typical of the way some young blokes like to talk between themselves about girls. It is often full of merely aspirational bravado. Nevertheless, that kind of talk trivialises women and girls and shows no respect for them as individuals or people with personalities. They tend to see girls as merely objects for a moment's sexual gratification and, sometimes, also simply a means of gaining kudos within their male social group. This is fairly common with some men of all ages who are in group situations. This toxic masculinity is a hang- over from the days of the 'wolf-whistle' but it has to be said that not all young men are like this. (And, nowdays, women also engage in such talk: "He's a gorgeous hulk!")

Yet, these three final-year Bachelor of Commerce students are not just aspirational about raping naïve girls. They've already gone beyond that on at least three previous occasions. Each of them has 'had' separate girls before by getting her almost blind drunk, taking her into the University gardens or even to the girl's own on-campus room, and having their way with her. Hugh has done it twice. So, they have been campus predators before and know how to go about it or think they do. Nevertheless, they are very cautious and work as a team when luring a girl. They like to notch up a tally of girls they've had and rating each girl as one to five stars for 'fuckability' or how well they enjoyed each girl, even though she may be drunk, flaked out or totally inebriated. In their tally, so- called "re-heats" are not to be counted, only "freshies". They are allowed to take trophies like knickers and bras. Each of these trophies can add an extra point to their overall score at the end of the year. They decide that oral sex before the real thing gets an extra point, too. At the suggestion of Hugh, the more egotistical of them, they adopt a rule that no condoms are allowed.

He told them: "Wearing a condom is like having a shower with your socks on." They laugh in agreement. He added: "I like my cunts raw. Going in with a naked dick gives you a real feel for the girl. When you thrust in, you know you're pushing into her meat. She's your's and no stupid bloody plastic bag's getting in the way."

More laughter. [13]

Hugh's mention of "her meat" typifies their attitude that the girls are nothing more than "meat". Also, Hugh spent one end of year vacation working at a meatworks. In the boning room as a knife hand, he had to cut up raw meat from very recently slaughtered cattle. Occasionally, that meat is still twitching.[14] So, his experience there and his view of young girls as just meat to be processed has relevance to him. Only with girls, there is also sexual arousal and gratification.

These three young final-year Commerce students came together as a team at the beginning of their second year and now, starting their final year, they resume their joint 'hobby'. Among some of the 'returner' students, they are known for being a rather silly group of pub drinkers and not taken seriously. Yet, they are worldly wise enough not to brag publicly and to just keep knowledge of their exploits between themselves. They are, of course, a secret group and this secrecy is part of what keeps them together and drives them.

Now, in their final year, they would like to escalate a tally in grand style before they graduate and go their separate ways. For this, they decide to focus on new 'fresher' first year students, looking out for those they see as shy and vulnerable.

Flash, is one of the 'Three Musketeers' from a farm in the west of Queensland, says: "Yeah, I'd like to cull a weaner heifer from the herd!"

Errol, from Kingaroy: "Yeah, I'll rope one an' give her the ride of her life!"

During the long summer break, one of them, Hugh the leader of the pack who is also a fitness enthusiast, was in Sydney. While there and after diligent enquiries,

---

[13] On this issue of 'banter boys talk Vs the real thing', see: Lee, D. & Kennelly, L. "Inside the Warwick University rape chat scandal." *BBC News*, London, 28 May 2019. https://www.bbc.com/news/uk-48366835

[14] The author has worked in the boning rooms of meat works in Queensland and in New Zealand. There, he has occasionally seen this 'twitching' or random nerve reflex action in meat of very recently killed beef just after it has come along the chain from the kill floor and, very rarely, even after the cut of beef has been removed from the carcass.

he was able to buy a single bubble card of 10 little grey/white oblong pills of *Rohypnol* on the blackmarket at Kings Cross, the infamous night life area of Sydney. It's the left overs from a larger box of 30 tablets.

Now back at University, he tells his mates about the pills and shows them the little tablets. He tells them that if sneaked into a drink they can make the drink fizz a little and if the drink is light in colour, such as a white wine, a tablet would give it a bluish tinge. It has a blue core

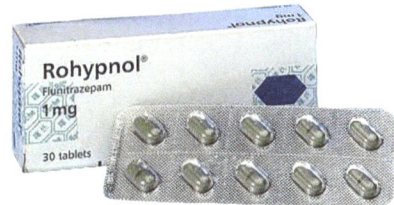

Rohypnol tablets which Hugh bought at Kings Cross in Sydney. (*Wikimedia*)

which when dissolved is designed to give a drink with a bluish colour as a warning sign. So, they must be careful and selective about which drinks to spike. The tablets must be used with a dark-coloured drink to disguise the bluish tinge. The mates are impressed with his knowledge and are eager to try it out. He tells them: "It can take up to 15 minutes for a girl to get all dizzy and floppy. Then, she ginna flake out for a couple of hours. That's cool 'coz, like, it also creates amnesia. So, she won't remember a fuckin' thing. When she wakes up she ginna have a bad headache but, an' this is the cool part, like I said, she won't remember a bloody thing, even from just before she had the pills. But, she'll know somebody has fucked her. Who? She won't have a fuckin' clue who it was. At the Cross they say that's when a girl has been 'roofied'."[15]

However, the randy Hugh has not yet had any conquests since returning from Sydney. So, he has not yet used any of these pills.

The three of them decide that they should work together as a team. After all, they are mates. Following further discussion over a few beers, they'll get a girl and give her a real good threesome 'gang bang'. That might be an enjoyable way to start their final year at University. And, they decide that after the 'gang bang' they'll each give the girl a rating of up to five stars.

Note: some of the following content may be confronting.

---

[15] 'Roofy' or 'roofied' is urban slang for *Rohypnol* or *Flunitrazepam*, a sedative that was made from the early 1970s and was used in hospitals only for deep sedation. It is now an infamous date-rape drug. See *Wikipedia* at https:// en.wikipedia.org/wiki/Flunitrazepam and at https://en.wikipedia.org/wiki/Date_rape_drug

During the third week of this first semester, they have firmed up on two fresher girls who they've noticed. Both girls are pretty, young looking and clearly new to the University scene and in their first year. Especially if they are country girls, they have a slightly naïve and bewildered look about them. One of girls attends a special Orientation activity for freshers interested in joining the Student Union operated Gym. This is when Hugh has noticed Cathy is wearing her room key on a small silver chain around her neck. He knows this is common practice as students don't like mislaying their key and being accidentally locked out of their room and having to get the residents hall manager to unlock it for them. Cathy was also warned by her mother to look after her key.

Hugh's seeing her key around her neck is one factor for why Cathy is the one they eventually select and concentrate on. They will have access to her room when she is 'roofied'. They won't have to gang rape her in the University's gardens.

Orientation Week, or just after it, is the most auspicious time to target unsuspecting first year girls. They would chat to the fresher girl and pretend to be a nice, kind, considerate, caring sort who respects girls. In the past, this tactic enabled them to successfully target three fresher girls last year. They would ply the girl with punch heavily laced with vodka. The 'Three Musketeers' were each able to lay a girl after getting her drunk in this way. They helped each other escort the inebriated girl to a place where one of them could have her. In two cases this was in the University's gardens. In the other case, the girl had her room key around her neck and knowing where her room was because the key had a number stamped on it, the threesome escorted her to he room. Then, two of them left while the third had his way. However, ten days later the girl reported the rape to the Police. Unfortunately, it was too late to collect DNA evidence and two weeks later the Police advised the girl that a prosecution had little chance of success. That is when the University Council made a move which was embargoed in the Council minutes. She was offered a $10,000 *ex gratia* payment and given assistance to transfer to a University in Brisbane with credit. In consultation with her parents, the girl accepted the University's offer.[16] The rapist ended up free to continue his studies but chose to transfer to another University in New South Wales.

By mid-year of their third year the two remaining 'Three Musketeers' had invited another student to restore their secret threesome. There is usually no shortage of young men willing to join in such exploits. He was the one who got the name 'Flash'.

However, not having had great success during this year's official Orientation Week, the 'Three Musketeers' decide to focus on one particular girl at a special 'Ides of March' party to be held on Saturday 17th of March for their first ever 'gang bang'. They hope she will be at this small informal party organised by a residential college. It is to be held in the recreational hall of the same residential college where Cathy lives in her room on the second floor. In fact, this will also be Cathy's seventeenth birthday. She keeps her birthday to herself. She is shy about being so young.

The 'Three Musketeers' go into action. Their *modus operandi* has usually been to each separately gain a targeted naïve girl's confidence and ply her with non-alcoholic drinks like 'lemon, lime and bitters' but liberally dosed with Vodka. Then, he would escort or even carry the inebriated girl off with help from his mates and then force himself upon her. But, this time they'll get the girl 'roofied' for their 'gang bang'. They are confident it'll be easier.

This party is ostensibly to celebrate the Ides of March which were actually a few days earlier. But, it's just an excuse for a party. The boys have noticed Cathy's room key around her neck. They know the number is stamped on it and they know the lay-out of the rooms.

---

[16] An actual case: during the early 1990s the author worked in a student support rôle at an Australian university. Across the corridor from his office was the Records section. One day during a shared lunch break, he was shown confidential University Council minutes. A female student had left the library when it closed at 10:00 p.m. and walked to her on campus accommodation. On the way, she was pulled behind some bushes and raped. She reported it to the Police who investigated. The outcome was that charges were dropped against the male student and the University agreed to pay the raped student a substantial *ex gratia* payment and arranged for her to be transferred to another university with credit provided that the rape received no publicity. The rapist came from a small regional town where his father was prominent in the community and was on the local shire council. The chairman of that shire council was also on the University Council. A positive outcome was that the University organised for a mini-bus shuttle service to collect students whenever the library closed and take them to their campus accommodation. Records section staff were deeply offended by the University's rôle but were locked by contract into silence.

The opposite of a social butterfly, Cathy is encouraged to come to the party by some friendly fellow female 'fresher' students just for a bit of fun "to lighten up your time here. There are some nice boys here who don't drink and chase women. And, they're good company." These girls are not connected to those lecherous Three Musketeers students and innocently encourage Cathy to join them simply for a fun evening.

At the party, most are quite mature students who have been at the University for a few years. And, there is some heavy drinking. So, Cathy feels a little out of her depth with all these older students. She is only just seventeen and is nervous about the alcohol around. She partially retreats to the edge of the party area. And as expected, she doesn't touch any alcohol. She has a long standing disdain for those who engage in party heavy drinking.

After around twenty minutes when most party goers are already there, the 'Three Musketeers' arrive together. They split up and begin to circle like a pack of predator hyenas on the Serengeti Plains. They go into action.

Hugh, is the leader among the group. On seeing Cathy alone like a wallflower, he walks up to her seemingly just to be friendly and hospitable towards a still timid 'fresher' now at the end of her third week.

Timid Cathy is nervous but pleased by a friendly face. They make small talk about the happy crowd.

Hugh says: "There's more people here than I expected. That's nice." He chats casually with Cathy.

It is all very reassuring for Cathy, as he chats charmingly with her for some time. He is quite flattering about her. He tells her he remembers her from the Orientation session at the Gym. Not socially very switched on, she is naïvely impressed. He tells her he likes being fit. He is slim, wiry and not tall. As Shakespeare said in his play *Julius Caesar*, "Yond Cassius has a lean and hungry look".[17] He definitely has a lecherous look about him rather like the goat characters and satyrs in some of Norman Lindsay's lusty etchings and

---

[17] Shakespeare, W. (about 1599), *Julius Caesar*, Act 1, Scene 2. Spoken by Mark Antony.

paintings.[18] In the example in the footnote below, the satyr is particularly hungry for the girl, as is Hugh. His appearance doesn't impress her but his seemingly kind and caring demeanour does. Moreover, when she inadvertently lets him know she's from a sheep grazing property near Guyra, he tells her he's from a cattle property near Charleville in Western Queensland, which is patently untrue. He may have visited Charleville at some time but he is actually from the inner Brisbane suburb of Annerley.

Cathy tries to impress this kindly older student. It is the nearest she has ever come to flirting. She tells him she has an inbuilt regard for country people. "Like you, they're the salt of the earth."

He has already detected her naïve attempt to ingratiate herself. He plays upon it. He describes life at Charleville, some of it imaginary. However, this still goes down well with naïve Cathy. He tells her he likes gymnastics as well as weight lifting, which he does. As the minutes pass, he gradually moves closer into her personal space. He is a skilled and experienced operator. He has used these kinds of lines before. Somehow, his pheromones have an effect on her. She is unconsciously receptive. Maybe, it is because she is in *oestrus*. But, she isn't yet fully aware that she is. She only started her periods two years ago but she knows about the signs in her cycles. She is a farm girl and has been around when a vet has been artificially inseminating (AI) ewes on the family property. However, we can be ruled by our hormones. And, pheromones act like hormones which we exude and sometimes very subtly influence our behaviour towards others and their behaviour towards us.[19] Anyway, whatever it is, the innocent and ingenuous now only just 17-year-old country girl come to town, Cathy, is taken in.

His two 'Musketeer' mates are watching and sniggering at a distance. Hugh then lightheartedly dares her to have some of the harmless punch: "It's alcohol free, just fruit juices, Coca Cola and some tiny bits of fruit in it."

---

[18] For example, his 1922 etching entitled *Bargains* at http://www.normanlindsay.net/Bargains.htm This same etching can be seen in Hope, A.D. (1976), *Siren and Satyr: the personal philosophy of Norman Lindsay*. Sun Books: Melbourne at page 16 along with many other of his gorgeous lascivious drawings. Copyright prevents its reproduction here.

[19] "Sex pheromone", *Wikipedia*. https://en.wikipedia.org/wiki/Sex_pheromone "Pheromones are chemicals capable of acting like hormones outside the body of the secreting individual, to impact the behaviour of the receiving individuals".

She knows it isn't totally non-alcoholic. Earlier on in the evening, others who mixed it told her that it had just a dash of Shiraz in it.[20]

But, being a red wine, it is actually ideal for the threesome's task with *Rohypnol* especially as the punch already has a sizeable base of Coca Cola and a dark colour. The blue tinge will not be noticed. And, the small amount of alcohol will probably add to the potency of the *Rohypnol*.

So, while Cathy knows it isn't completely non-alcoholic, she is still impressed by this third year student's apparent politeness and chivalry. He's a country bloke, too. In a happy and re- assured mood, she is persuaded to be daring and have some of the punch. She thinks to herself: 'I have red wine at Holy Communion on Sundays anyway. So, what's the big deal. It's only a small part diluted in a fruity punch. And, after all it's my birthday. I can celebrate!'

So, feeling happier, she doesn't worry and is still positive and almost admires this young man's conduct, she tells him very quietly: "Actually, nobody else knows, but today is my birthday. I'm seventeen, now."

Hugh: "Wow! … I wouldn't have guessed. You don't look seventeen. More like sweet sixteen! Well, even more reason to have some punch."

Cathy smiles at him.

She has been snared.

Hugh doesn't try to congratulate her with a hug. He suspects she would back off instantly with that close contact. He wants to keep her on side.

So, he very politely fetches her a glass of punch. On the way back to her, he pops three of his little pills into the drink. (He doesn't know that this makes this drink a bit of an overdose.[21]) At first, it fizzes a bit but it is fairly dark where they are talking and, with the Coca Cola base in the punch, it would naturally be a little fizzy and even have a dark colour. So, the drink doesn't obviously have the bluish colour which it would normally have as a legally required warning.

---

[20] Shiraz is a red wine.

[21] "Rohypnol Fast Facts", *United States Department of Justice*, 01 January 2006. https://www.justice.gov/archive/ndic/pubs6/6074/index.htm Each of Hugh's tablets is 1mg. 2mg is an adult dose. 3mg is an overdose.

Soon, she is feeling feint and a little dizzy. Being early March, it is still warm and the air- conditioning is struggling to keep up with the crowd. It needs turning up. He tells her: "Have a little more to drink. That'll help."

She is trusting this older student. Feeling warm, she does have some more.

Then, he tells her: "Come outside into the fresh air."

She is compliant but says: "I'm feeling a little dizzy."

He leads her outside onto the long verandah. As they go out of the French doors, he turns momentarily and smiles at his two mates, briefly raising his fist as a signal rather like an old steam engine driver sounding the locomotive's whistle.[22] They look around to see if anyone is watching. It is crowded and no one is. They follow at a safe distance. Now outside, Cathy's speech becomes slurred and broken.

---

[22] This gang rape of Cathy has some resemblance to what used to happen at Ingham in North Queensland during the 1970s. Stannard, B., Hanford, B. and Summers, A. "How women are trained", in Pullan, R. (Ed.) (1985), *The Way We Are*. Sydney: Allen & Unwin, pages 113-134. Ingham is a small town of 4,500 people in north Queensland with an economy based on sugar cane farming. Sometimes, at a local party girls were enticed outside and subsequently taken away and gang raped. Some girls as young as 12 were gang raped and some 13-year-olds became pregnant and the father could have been any number of young blokes living in Ingham. Some girls' parents tried to take legal action but were thwarted by the boys' fathers who were in high places in the community and had contacts in the police. In those days stupefying pills like *Rohypnol* were generally unknown. Alcohol was the preferred method in the 1970s. But, in Ingham it was simply abduction and gang rape followed by threats of severe beatings afterwards if reported or if further rapes were not accepted by the girl. The researchers saw this as how girls were trained in a typical small town.

In one of many Ingham cases where girls had become pregnant after a gang rape, when one girl walked down the main Lannercost Street on a Saturday morning with her baby in a pram, she was followed by a small group of young men who taunted her with "which one of us is yer kid's daddy?" (Page 126) In the 1970s and 1980s there was no DNA testing available to determine parentage. And, Ingham, with a large Italian-origin population, is very Catholic. Therefore, abortion was not only very illegal but socially unacceptable. These Ingham gang rapes were focussed on by those authors to study Australian small town sexual activities among young people.

See also: Ross, G. & Schulz, J. "Girls in our town just haven't a chance." *Gamut* 1977. https:// espace. library.uq.edu.au/data/UQ_252071/GAMUT_1977_47_2.pdf?E Gang raped girls are threatened with more of the same if they go to the Police. Girls as young as 12 have been brutally pack raped and threatened into accepting that their role is to supply favours for young blokes. Being sexually abused by young men was a form of social acceptance.

The misogyny rife in Ingham in the 1970s is the same which drives these men at Cathy's university: girls are solely for the sexual pleasure of men. Thus, in some ways what they and those Ingham young men used to do is reminiscent of a more recent sexual conquest game played by a young Australian cricketer in England and his friends: "Rape victim 'humiliated by Australian cricketer's game of sexual conquest'." *News at Nine*, Sydney, 22 May 2019. https:// www.9news.com.au/world/uk-news-alex-hepburn-joe-clarke-cricketer-rape-whatsapp/8b2379b2-5d51-421e-8f5e- befef4f76c203?ocid=edm-nine.com.au-ninedaily--190522&mktg_scr=edm-ninedaily Also reported in England: Adnitt, J., "Alex Hepburn: Rape victim 'humiliated by sexual conquest game'." *BBC Derbyshire*, 21 May 2019 https:// www.bbc.com/news/uk-england-hereford-worcester-48339099 Some of his *WhatsApp* messages to his mates were: "Get them blind and then back to ours" and "I reckon I'm about 75. I want 20 more this summer."

These conquest games are not unusual. See: "Spur Posse" in *Wikipedia* at https://en.wikipedia.org/wiki/Spur_Posse

Again, he urges her to have some more to drink. "That'll help cool you."

Still trusting, she drinks some more. She has almost finished the glass.

He tells her: "Here, finish it up." She does.

Then, she can't stand up properly. She is feeling very dizzy. Her speech is slurred. She asks: "Where am I?"

He tells her: "I'll take you to your room. You'll feel better there."

The other two blokes rush in to help him prop her up. Her key is exactly where they expected it to be, on the silver chain around her neck. As Hugh looks at the key around her neck, he tells them: "It's room 219!"

They look back into the party hall and tell Hugh: "Nobody's watching."

As they escort her away, Hugh: "Good. ... Ya know, she told me it's her birthday today. So, we ginna give her a big birthday present!"

The others snigger nervously.

One of them: "Wow! Can't wait to go through her."

As the leader, Hugh tells them: "Don't forget, I'm goin' first."

He thinks to himself: 'She's my virgin. I wanna break into her myself. An' I don't wanna go in on other fellas' slops.'

The three of them virtually carry her upstairs in the dark via the fire escape so that they are not seen leading her away. She is taken to her room on the second floor. They don't even have to remove the key from around her neck as they hold her close to the door handle.

CHAPTER 3

Cathy traumatised

Nearly seven hours later, Cathy wakes up slowly. She has had a large dose. It is still before sunrise and dark on this Sunday morning. But, the main bedroom light is on and bright for her. Her mouth is dry. She is lying uncovered and totally naked on her bed, legs slightly apart, aching in the groin, thirsty, dizzy, nauseous and with a big headache. She is bruised around her breasts, neck, and thighs. Her *mons pubis* area (the rounded part just above the vulva) is sore and feels bruised.

She sits up. Her head is really aching. Her room key is on the chain around her neck.

Her clothes are roughly scattered on the floor.

She picks up a hand held mirror from her bedside table and looks at herself. She looks a mess. Her hair is all tousled. She examines her groin with the hand-held mirror. She notices there are some small bite marks at her upper thighs close to her vulva and on one of her outer labia. Her clitoris is sore and feels bruised. She is also bleeding a little from her vagina. She is shocked not just by the bleeding and bruising but, as she looks closer, because she is now sitting up, there is now semen oozing out of her. (Having helped her father with rams for AI or Artificial Insemination purposes, she knows what semen looks like.) To her horror, she realises that somebody has had sex with her and in doing so they have done many things to her. And, she notices that there is a small 2mm tear at her perineum at about the 6:35 p.m. point. "What has been done to me?!!!"

She can hardly even remember going to the party. Her arrival at the party is only very hazy in her mind. She doesn't remember people she talked to there.

Cathy's shock and horror is profound.

She stands up and looks at herself in the wardrobe mirror. She is a bit unsteady. There are also some 'love bite' marks on her neck close to her shoulders. She is even more shocked. A little blood and some more semen start slowly running down one of her inner thighs. She tries wiping it away with tissue paper. More comes out. Actually, quite a lot. (There were three virile men.)

In confused panic, shame and disgust she has a long shower, washing herself thoroughly. After she has dressed herself in clean clothes, she collects up the dress she wore last night and strips the sheets and bed cover off the bed (there is no blanket as it is still summer). She bundles up those items and puts them in two large plastic bags. But, she can't find the knickers she wore. And, where's her bra? That's gone, too. She realises that they must have been taken as souvenirs. Shocked and disgusted, she quietly takes the plastic bags of bundled-up clothes and bed linen downstairs and puts them in an industrial bin or dumpster near the kitchen back door. It is still early in the morning. In an hour or so, the rubbish truck will come on its daily early morning round and will empty the bin. All this is exactly what Police say a rape victim should NOT do. They need DNA evidence. She has just washed it all away in the shower and got rid of that which she couldn't wash away.

Yet, *Rohypnol* can be detected in a victim's urine and blood for more than 24 hours. So, it would still have helped if she went to the Police. They are good at finding DNA traces on places like door handles and table tops and even from hair unknowingly dropped on carpets. But, shame and disgust hold her back. During the next few days she has frequent showers to cleanse her body.

This morning she is too ashamed to go downstairs to the dining hall for breakfast. She does not want to be seen. And, she is worried that whoever did this to her might see her. Instead, she spends all day Sunday in her room. She only eats a few crackers from a packet she left on her dressing table some time ago. She doesn't even go to Church, something she rarely misses on Sundays. She is very depressed.

Eventually, on Monday morning she comes out of her room. She is hungry and has breakfast in the dining hall.

Sitting alone she is thinking: 'Shall report this to the Police? No. I'm too ashamed. But, I know I'll get better. I'm a farm girl. I know the female body heals quickly down there. I've seen ewes just days after birth and I didn't give birth.'

Still alone at her dining table and cupping her face in her hands: 'No, I can't report. I don't know who he is. I can't remember anything. What'll everyone say? How can I tell Mother and my Dad? I don't want it to affect my studies … and my enrolment here. And, Police will ask questions.'

A girl sees her distress and sits down next to her.

She asks: "You alright, dear?"

Cathy looks up. She's never seen the girl before but she looks kind: "I think I've been raped … but I can't remember anything … I think I've been drugged."

The helpful girl puts her arm around Cathy's shoulder. Then, she tells her: "I know someone just over there who can help. I'll go and get her."

She walks over to a distant table and talks to another student.

They both walk over to Cathy and sit down with her.

Cathy is sobbing quietly.

The first girl says to Cathy: "This is Elizabeth Melrose. She's Chair of our Women's Network and she's a Law student. Please tell her about it."

The second girl introduces herself: "Hi. Would you like to tell me about what happened? I may be able to help. That's only a 'maybe', though."

Suddenly pleased somebody has offered help, Cathy starts spilling the beans to her.

The first girl quietly leaves with a parting word: "Hang in there, dear."

After listening in silence, Elizabeth tells Cathy quite frankly: "Listen, please. I'm in fourth year Law. I'll tell you where you stand. It's not good news. First of all, you've told me you don't have any idea who he was. Of course, he would have left DNA evidence around either in you or on your body or you clothes or even just the door handle. But, you've got rid of most of that. So, you know, because you now have little evidence, the Police will probably give you the third degree. You won't like it. Yes, it's just not fair. You don't need all that right now. Some people could say you even invited him into your room and you wanted sex. That's not fair, too. His lawyer will say you consented. The lawyer will say he asked you an' you said nuthin'. So, their lawyer will say that's consent, even though you were flaked out, ya know 'blotto'. He'll say he didn't know you were 'blotto'. He'll say you just wanted get on with it an' lay there waiting for him. Yeah, being 'blotto' is like putting out the 'welcome mat', if you see what I mean."

Cathy is astounded at the frankness, the language and the rationale used. It shows on her face. "How can they say that?!!"

Elizabeth, the Law student, gently: "Listen to me. You've told me you're from from New South Wales. This is Queensland, dearie. As I said, I'm in my final year of Law. The law about consent is different here. The Court could be persuaded that you consented by your silence. The lawyers all know about that legal strategy. An' this fella what had ya that night of the party, well, he probably knows about that, too.[23] It would be humiliating for you. That argument can hold up in Court even if, in fact, you were unconscious because there is now no evidence that you were drugged and right out of it. In fact, because of this ridiculous law, the Police might even pressure you not to proceed with a complaint because the unlikelihood of success. In other words, they might see you as wasting Police time if you persisted."

Cathy is silent. The real world is hitting her.

The friendly Law student continues: "An, ya know, that bastard whoever he is, well, he'll wanna shut you up. Like, put blame on you. Fair dinkum, his lawyers will."

After a moment's silence and as what she has told Cathy begins to sink in, Elizabeth adds: "Yeah, they could make life hell for you ... an' the Police could, too. Ya gotta be so careful, dearie. Oh dear, I feel for ya. I 'spose it's a big lesson for ya."

She puts her hand on Cathy's hands.

---

[23] Unfortunately for Cathy, Elizabeth is blunt but largely correct. Gleeson, H., "Mistake of fact defence: The legal loophole stopping Queensland rape complainants from getting justice." *ABC News*, Brisbane, 13 May 2019. https:// www.abc.net.au/news/2019-05-13/bri-lee-mistake-of-fact-campaign-queensland-sexual-consent/11095306

Also: Wolfe, N., "The few seconds and hair touch that let a rapist go free" *News.com* 10 July 2019. https://www.news.com.au/national/queensland/courts-law/the-few-seconds-and-hair-touch-that-let-a-rapist-go-free/news-story/ceecea73968b729569d376b5523ef3df

Note: That was the situation in 2018 when Cathy was drugged and raped. Queensland laws have now caught up with the rest of Australia. "What is consent". https://www.qld.gov.au/community/getting-support-health-social-issue/support-victims-abuse/sexual-abuse-assault/lets-talk-sexual-consent/sexual-consent-explained

"That fella who did this to you doesn't care a stuff about you. In your condition your body was his to do what he wanted an' how he wanted, ya know being kinky and even rough. That's probably why you've got those bruises. And, you know there might have been more than one bloke. If there was, they may have taken turns. They may have even photographed you being raped. From what you've told me, I think you've been 'roofied' ".

Cathy: "What's that?"

"Your drink has been spiked with something called *Rohypnol,* very hard to notice in your drink. You wouldn't know a bloody thing 'coz, like, ya weren't just drunk.

The predatory 'Hugh' is leader of the pack. (Posed by model)

Nah, you were 'roofied' or 'blotto' like totally unconscious from a tablet they secretly dissolved in your drink."

Cathy asks: "Is that 'roofied'?

Elizabeth: "Yes. … Then, when you were blotto, he or they could have done all sorts of things to you like love bites, licking you, or putting a finger up you and so on."

Shocked silence from Cathy. She is gobsmacked and deeply, deeply humiliated at the obscenely intrusive use of her body. She thinks to herself: 'I've seen cattle dogs licking a bitch when she comes on heat. But, with humans, yeeurk!' She just knows nothing about oral sex.

She is not only really, really shocked, she is beside herself with worry.

Cathy thinks: 'So, that's why I'm so bruised. He … or they did all those things to me? I've heard of 'date rape' but I've never really understood what it is. Have I been 'date raped'? By more than one? Couldn't happen to me. I don't hang around pubs. At St Agnes School I didn't climb the fence and go to Surfers Paradise. I don't go to wild parties. No, couldn't happen to me.'

Because of what this student has said, a very confused Cathy now even asks herself: 'Did I ask them to my room? Did I ask them to … No, I wouldn't have. But, could I have? Could I have?' She is now plagued by doubt. She starts crying.

In genuine sympathy, the Elizabeth squeezes both Cathy's hands. She tells her: "You told me you couldn't find your underwear. I think your suspicious are right. They've probably been taken as a souvenir or a trophy."

Cathy's tearful response: "Yeeerk! That's horrible!"

Elizabeth tells her more: "Unfortunately, you have destroyed the evidence needed to support your case in Court: the clothes and bed linen. And, of course you showered. And, that was two days ago. The proof has gone. So, you see, if you go to the Police or anyone else, it could be so humiliating, embarrassing, and degrading for you. The rapist or at least his lawyer knows how to get him off with that legal loophole which prevents Queensland rape complainants getting justice. It's what they call a

Cathy with supportive Elizabeth. (*Dreamstime.* Posed by models)

'Mistake of fact defence'. And, without the evidence which you discarded, it would be an uphill battle for your legal team. I'm not trying to put you down. I'm a woman and a final year Law student and I know this part of the law. It's stacked against you. The law will eventually change. There's no doubt about that. Queensland will soon fall in line with other states."[24]

Thoughts are running through Cathy's mind.

She asks: "I live in New South Wales. Does that make any difference?"

"I'm afraid not. The crime happened in Queensland under Queensland jurisdiction. It would have to be tried here under Queensland law."

Elizabeth gives Cathy a business card. "Look, I can't practice Law yet but I can commiserate with you and can even refer you. And look, I'm also Chair of the University Students Association's Women's Network. When you feel like it, I would welcome you to our meetings. See, this card tells you when we meet. There are others in the Group with similar experiences. You are not alone. You will get genuine support. I promise you that."

This is all too much for Cathy. In floods of tears, she takes the card, suddenly gets up, and rushes back to her room in her residential college. There, she looks up

---

[24]   See previous footnote about changes to Queensland law.

'date rape' on the internet, especially at *Wikipedia*. She realises how naïve she has been. Why didn't she see it coming? She should never have gone to that party. Yet, she can't remember anything about it. She just vaguely remembers dressing for it and then arriving. Everything is blank until she woke up. 'Oh God, the things he did to me! Or, was it the things they did to me! Did they take photos! Oh, my God!'

Yet again, she has a shower, thoroughly washing her groin area.

She is so upset and feeling so alone. She spends hours lying on her bed. Occasionally, she wails in distress. She turned seventeen only two days ago. She is still a very young and simple country girl who has been exploited because of her naïvety.

Distraught Cathy in her room.
(*iStockphoto*. Posed by model)

Cathy now begins many months of alternating between strong feelings of shame, guilt and disgust on the one hand and deep simmering but growing anger on the other. But, until the end of the current academic year the shame is with her all the time. Elizabeth has vividly and brutally made her aware of sex that she simply could not have imagined in her prudish outlook on life. And, she has let her know how it could have been used with such indecency and wanton lechery to violate and abuse her unconscious body.

Cathy tries but can't really imagine why and how young men could do all those things to her. The idea that one or several unknown men bit her in very private places, licked her, and even put their finger in her is just abhorrent to her. And, uninvited, they pumped their semen into her. These thoughts send a cold shiver down her spine: "Yeurk!" She is devastated.

Nevertheless, this rape changes Cathy. Not only has her awareness of it and now her newly acquired knowledge of the sex involved ended her innocence, but it has created a growing profound anger. As time passes, the anger gets stronger and more dominant. Yet, she still keeps it all to herself. Apart from Elizabeth Melrose and, very briefly that first helpful girl, she tells nobody, not even her mother or father. As a loner, she bottles it up and suffers in silence.

Just two weeks later, Cathy's mother arrives in the family Toyota Prado to take her home for the short mid-semester break and for Easter. She mentions nothing of the gang rape to her Mother or when they get home to her Father. She hopes and expects it to all wash off. Meanwhile, she'll just lie low. Anyway, the family is about to have a late celebration of her seventeenth birthday. She doesn't want to spoil things.

CHAPTER 4

A Parasite

Now, with her home for the mid-semester break, she has a late birthday celebration party on one of the verandahs of the lovely old house. Held on Saturday the 7th of April, it is a quiet private party which includes the farm manager and his wife. Her parents give her a lovely brand new white Kia Cerato hatchback. She is so pleased, not just with the lovely little car but with the independence it will give her. She is a happy girl.

At this point Cathy is also reminded by her father that the Medibank Private shares they bought for her seventeen years ago are now hers because she has turned seventeen. He suggests she hangs onto them, because they have grown in value to over $300,000. She should always reinvest the annual interest.

She doesn't realise it, but she is actually a spoilt little rich girl! She's been born with a silver spoon in her mouth. She tends to think all this largesse from parents is normal.

Then, while at home at 'Hampton Downs' and nearly four weeks after the rape she starts having morning sickness. It takes a few days for her to realise what it is. Initially, she thought she had a stomach bug. She was in Guyra a day ago and had a lovely Chinese meal with her parents. This was the night before returning to University in her lovely new car.

The day after arriving back at University it started, she spoke to her mother on the phone. Her Mother told her: "We won't have Chinese again. They don't cook their vegetables long enough."

(*Depositphotos.*
Posed by model)

After a few more days, the morning nausea and some vomiting persist. Now, she realises what they really mean. She knows why she has missed a period. She is pregnant.[25]

To be certain, she goes to a chemist shop in Toowoomba and buys a pregnancy test kit. This confirms her worst fears. Now, she is even more upset and worried. There are support facilities and counsellors at each residential hall at the University. But, she doesn't know what to do about it. Who could she tell? Who could she talk to? How could she talk to her mother on the phone? She would tear her to shreds. She would drive up to Toowoomba and make a big public fuss. Then, she thinks or hopes the shame and disgust will just pass and she'd get over it. She didn't expect pregnancy. After all, this was her first and only sexual interaction, ever. The first ever! How could that happen!?! Not likely. The test result must be an error. Maybe her natural hormones during *oestrous* made her receptive to accommodating that man's or those blokes' advances? Did her natural pheromones released during *oestrous* lead them on? Is she guilty of encouraging her rapists, like Elizabeth said the perpetrator's lawyer might say? She does a lot of this introspection. Would a counsellor at the University believe she didn't encourage them. Would a counsellor believe she didn't want sex? No, she won't go to a student counsellor. This is what she is thinking.

But, what has happened was simply not her fault. She was drugged with *Rohypnol.* While she was unconscious, it was clearly 'date rape' and a gang version, too. She is very muddled. She is a young only just seventeen-year-old conservative country girl on her own in a strange and harsh world who has found herself in dire straits.

The morning sickness is mainly in the mornings and lasts for a month before tailing off. That is when she thinks the pregnancy was just her imagination, possibly

---

[25]   In a recent article in the American academic journal *Human Nature* it was estimated that rapes are twice as likely to result in pregnancies than with consensual sex. "Are per-incident rape-pregnancy rates higher than per-incident consensual pregnancy rates?". *Human Nature*. March 2003, 14 (1): Pages 1–20. https://link.springer.com/article/ 10.1007%2Fs12110-003-1014-0 (This is an abstract. The conclusion in the main article is quite plain about this.)

a false pregnancy? She looks it up on the internet and finds a site dealing with false positive test results.[26] Maybe, a false positive result was caused by the upset tummy from the Chinese food. She makes all sorts of excuses like these. While increasingly worried, she stoically and diligently keeps up her lectures, tutorials and assignment work.

During four weeks of morning sickness, she misses just two lectures because of the nausea and vomiting. However, she continues to alternate between depression and anger about what has happened with anger coming to the fore more often, especially now that she realises she is probably pregnant. Yet, she is so stubbornly private about it. She makes up her mind to tell no one. She obdurately will not see a doctor. It's almost as if she still hopes the test result was false and it'll go away. She puts it down to experience, an experience she'd rather not have had.

Yet, she still worries about not having a period for so long, now. Is there something wrong with her? Should she see a doctor? She puts it off, now hoping her menstrual cycle will kick in again soon.

Finally, one morning after a shower and looking at herself in the mirror, she accepts the fact that she is pregnant. Her tummy is just beginning to swell and harden-up, too. So, she decides that with this growing tummy, she needs privacy. She will move off campus, into a small unit and live by herself. So, she doesn't rent a unit near the University. No, she buys one and it's right in the centre of town. After selling some of her Medibank Private shares, she buys a modern two bedroom unit. No mortgage, no bank approval, just cash upfront. And, after a building inspection,

there is no 28 day waiting period. It is a long way from the University. It is a small modern unit in town in Clifford Street opposite the Grand Central shopping mall in the middle of Toowoomba. It's a good buy and will more than retain its value. There is also a security gate at the front access from the street. So, she feels safe here. Now, she

Cathy's unit with the Kia Cerato parked at the front. It is opposite the big shopping mall.

---

[26] "7 Causes for a False-Positive Pregnancy Test", 2020, *Healthline*, https://www.healthline.com/health/pregnancy/ false-positive-pregnancy-test

can be really private and only drive to University for lectures and tutorials. She will be the anonymous girl who simply comes and goes to Uni without lingering. Nobody will notice her and her growing bump. And, she can concentrate on her studies.

To start this new page in her life, Cathy has a hair cut. Her below shoulder hair in plaits has gone. Her hair is now just collar length. She feels it makes her look different and more mature. She hopes she is no longer so noticeable with this more ordinary hair style.

However, she assumed she would be private living in her new unit. In fact, where she starts living now, she is noticed despite her shorter hair. Young men and older men try to engage with her and come knocking on her door. A man in his forties brings flowers and asks her out. She is cool towards him, declining the flowers and the offer of an outing. He is obviously disappointed and walks away dejected. Others also try to chat her up. She is so attractive and her belly is only just beginning to swell slowly. It is hardly noticeable until she is more than six months into the pregnancy, although she is very self-conscious about it. For some men, her attractiveness lies in her little girl appearance. She senses it. She is beginning to hate the advances of these men. "Can't they leave me alone!" So, she withdraws even more.

Finally, Cathy senses that her little girl appearance is attractive to men, especially older men. So, hoping to put them off, she has her plaited hair cut shorter to collar length. This doesn't make any difference. They are still attracted to her, probably even more so. But, they don't realise this 'little girl' is already very pregnant. (*Depositphotos*. Posed by model)

She starts wearing big loose fitting dresses, not just to hide the pregnancy but to cover herself up more. At the University, the few people who interact with her tend to think she is just going through an alternative life-style stage or perhaps it is her increasing feminism.

Cathy stubbornly will not seek help. She'll battle this out herself. Yet, the University has a counselling service very capable of looking after students like her. They can even arrange a safe and legitimate abortion. And, there would be absolute and total confidentiality. Her parents would never know. And, it would be free. She is not really aware of all this because she has deliberately isolated herself and is stubbornly persisting with her self-reliance.

Soon, she is beginning to develop a strong loathing for all men, especially young men. She is no longer blaming herself, her hormones or her pheromones. Now, she won't sit next to any male student at lectures and doesn't interact with any at tutorials. Sometimes, she thinks she knows who the rapist was or who those rapists were but is never sure. Her anger is now blaming all young men. It is a developing misandry. And, this attitude is increasingly incorporated into and included in her studies and assignments at University.

Despite her wearing those loose fitting almost hippy-style long dresses, she still goes for sometimes quite long jogs in the early morning, usually several kilometres. In central Toowoomba, this puts her at risk. During early June she is attacked in broad daylight while jogging. It is about 6:30 a.m. and along the western end of Margaret Street near Laurel Bank Park and still a little dark. She is nearly home when a man seems to be also jogging and catching up to her. Near a bus stop at an entrance to the park he suddenly lunges at her, hoping to bring her down in a rugby style tackle. Cathy, sensing danger, briefly turns sideways, sees him as he prepares to tackle her and kicks out at him, connecting him in the face. He turns and bolts. His attack failed. Shaken, she heads straight home to her unit. Distraught, she cries and cries. How she hates men.

So, following this attack and because of her growing bump, she backs off from early morning jogging in the street, instead jogging in the late afternoon. She is fearful of her bump being noticed. But, she is super vigilant and actively steers clear of men in the street. Fortunately, nothing happens during her afternoon jogging.

She still doesn't know who the rapist or rapists at University were and doesn't want to ask anyone. But, she once heard giggling comments in the row of seats behind her in a lecture theatre. She has heard talk that it was three different blokes which reinforces what Elizabeth told her was a possibility. Then, she even overhears some students walking behind her, male and female, giggling about her situation as they all walk to a lecture: "which one of them blokes is the father?" Again, this confirms her worst fears which she now tends to accept that it was more than one rapist.

As the pregnancy progresses, she continues wavering between shame and anger about herself and what was done to her. Anger increasingly dominates as does her stubborn resolve to see out her problem by herself. Yet, she is also more and more worried about what to do about her situation. She diligently concentrates on her studies and her music practice as a kind of escape. Yet, Cathy has absolutely no ante-natal care or advice. But, as a farm girl she knows a bit about reproduction and believes she can handle it on her own. After all, she has helped her father during lambing when ewes have needed help. And, after the rape she didn't have tests for sexually transmitted diseases. Her stubborn mixture of denial, guilt and anger has not done her any good.

At five months, her pregnancy is only just beginning to show at her lower abdomen, as in this photo. Her fit belly is usually flat. This is when she starts wearing loose fitting long dresses. (*Depositphotos*. Posed by model)

She was a virgin until the gang rape. Although private about it, inwardly she used to be almost even proud of it, too. Now, she is both humiliated and very angry. She doesn't want what those rapists did to her to get the better of her. Nevertheless, she believes she is stoic, tough and made of strong values. She continues going to Church on most Sundays where she prays for God's help. She persists with her classes.

At the end of the first semester in mid-June, she is 14 weeks pregnant but with her dresses she has been disguising it quite well. Though, she is so very self-conscious about it. She drives home to the family property 'Hampton Downs', north of Guyra. But, it ends up as just a quick two- day visit. Usually, she would spend the whole three-week mid-year break at home. She was going to tell her parents about what has happened and ask them for help, maybe even ask to have an abortion arranged, something she would normally in principle be totally against even though it would still be legal. She is going through an angry phase about her predicament. She even finds herself distancing herself from her father because he is male.

She keeps telling herself that she needs to get rid of this parasite living in her: "a parasite that some bloody misogynist put in me!" (Even a mild swear word like 'bloody' is not usual for Cathy.) But, she doesn't get a chance to tell her parents. They are busy. But, what really puts her off telling them is what her mother says shortly after her arrival home. Her conservative mother comments: "My dear, your tastes in clothes have become a bit hippy. It's those big floppy full- length dresses. They don't look good. They're not you. And, your hair is short. I suppose it'll grow back. Are you becoming a feminist, now? I wish you'd wear something more appropriate. I suppose, at least, it's not mini-skirts. Anyway, you can't help around the property dressed like that - so impractical. How would you mount a horse?"

This upsets Cathy but she doesn't show it. She just smiles.

Next day, she makes an excuse related to her studies and drives back to her unit at Toowoomba. She feels let down by her family. She is upset and cries a lot during the journey. She spends the rest of the second semester furiously concentrating on her studies. She loves and is inspired by her Music studies. Her ability on the piano is recognised by staff.

However, eventually she does go to see the University's student health doctor. At the Toowoomba University Health Service desk she asks for an appointment to see somebody about "Women's Health". She adds: "It must be a woman doctor." Two days later, while telling the doctor about her pregnancy, she does not mention the rape. She is too ashamed and embarrassed.

The kindly doctor examines her: "Now, am I correct in saying that from what I've seen, you've not given birth before?"

Cathy gives her a curt reply: "Never!"

Slightly taken aback, the doctor asks when she thinks the baby was conceived.

Cathy answers strongly: "Saturday night 17th of March! That was the only time. I've never had sex before or after! The misogynist rats!"

Her fists are tightly clenched. The doctor: "Oh dear."

Not knowing quite how to be compassionate with this suddenly very angry young girl, she gently holds Cathy's fists as a supportive gesture. Then, she even helps Cathy dress.

Cathy relaxes a little.

The doctor gets her to sit down.

She then looks at the diary on her desk, opens it at a calendar and does a quick count of the weeks. "Well, I would say you're almost exactly 19 weeks from conception. From feeling your tummy, I think that at this stage the pregnancy is progressing normally. And, your weight and fitness stand you in good stead."

She smiles at Cathy who is still not feeling relaxed with this caring woman.

Cathy: "That's what I calculated, too. You see, I know the exact date and the time it happened. It was around 10:00 p.m. on Saturday 17th of March. I was a virgin. I never had sex before that and I haven't since."

The doctor holds Cathy's hands again. Politely and not wanting to be intrusive, she doesn't ask about the circumstances.

Cathy continues: "And, I think that was nearly three weeks after my last period. My cycles usually had a slightly late ovulation. I could tell by my feelings and the mucus in my pants. At ovulation there were usually clear and wet secretions for the three to four days. I understand that is what happens two or three days before and during ovulation.[27] But, this time nothing happened.

Not the usual mucus. So, I suspected I must have just missed an ovulation. I was hoping my regularity was being irregular, if you see what I mean. Then, four weeks later I started morning sickness. So, I bought a pregnancy test kit at the chemist. Well, I knew then. But, I still hoped the test was wrong. I hoped it was a 'false positive'."

The doctor, still holding Cathy's hands: "Well, missed ovulation and that test, together they're reliable indicators. Now, I've sensed your anger and upset. So, I'm asking you do you want this pregnancy to go to term? Do you want to become a mother?"

Cathy's curt response: "No, I don't! Not now!"

The doctor: "Well, have you considered a termination?"

Cathy: "Do you mean an abortion?"

---

[27] This is the "Billings Method". See: "Cervical mucus method for natural family planning". *Mayo Clinic*, Arizona, USA. https://www.mayoclinic.org/tests-procedures/cervical-mucus-method/about/pac-20393452

Cathy is not Catholic but she is a committed 'High Church' Anglican[28] and regards abortion as immoral and a sin.

The doctor: "Well, you're over sixteen and legally don't need parental permission. And, at 19 weeks it is still perfectly legal.[29] With specialist care organised by this the University's Health Centre, it is free. It would be over within an hour and you could go home shortly after … provided that there are … ."

Stubborn and anachronistic Cathy: "No!"

She stood up to go.

The doctor: "Look, here's my card. Give me a ring if you want to talk it over some more. There is no way that I would put pressure on you either way."

Cathy: "No thank you."

What flashes through her mind now is the idea that abortion is a death, a real death of a living human. She is torn between her ethics and her anger.

She storms out.

In August, Cathy attends a public lecture at the University given by a visiting feminist, Dale Spender[30]. On entering the lecture theatre, Elizabeth Melrose spots her and comes to great her. Cathy is taken aback, almost bowled over by the warm reception given by Elizabeth. She loves the lecture and is inspired by the arguments against our patriarchal society. She found she loves it when Dale Spender picked on hapless men in the audience and humiliated them.[31] After the lecture, she again meets up with Law student Elizabeth Melrose and joins the Student Union Women's Network which had organised Spender's visit. With her conservative squattocracy background,

---

[28] See "High church" in *Wikipedia* at https://en.wikipedia.org/wiki/High_church
    This *YouTube* item exemplifies Cathy's views on abortion and protecting life: https://www.youtube.com/watch?v=AxGpm4j0xhw&list=PL7p2AAcz9AHgu2S2ViPizFeHCwLj2woUK However, we will later see that under stress she does not exactly practice what as a good Anglican she believes. She sees the baby she has just given birth to as a 'parasite', a view not uncommon among rape victims in Congo Kinshasa and in Rohingya refugee camps. She abandons it to die. However, a few hours after the birth she suddenly has a different perspective in a dreamlike situation where she is grateful that the baby is being saved. She imagines divine intervention. In fact, the baby is saved.

[29] At section 5 in the *Termination of Pregnancy Act of 2018*, an abortion may be legally procured before 22 weeks if performed by a registered medical practitioner.

[30] See *Wikipedia* at https://en.wikipedia.org/wiki/Dale_Spender Dale Spender died in 2023 five years after the setting of this story.

[31] The author once attended one of Dale Spender's public lectures. Fortunately, he missed being picked on.

this is something she would never have dreamed of doing before. Then, shortly after joining the group and a week after Dale Spender's lecture, she goes to a hairdresser in town and has a much shorter pageboy style haircut. Anger is increasingly driving her.

In September during the mid-semester break she does not drive home. She makes an excuse about her piano playing and needs to practice with the local choral society. But, she is very, very worried. Her pregnancy is finally getting the better of her. In the stress of being alone and so worried, she spends much mid-semester vacation time alone in her unit.

She was very relieved by the first rate scores she got for her courses at the end of the first semester. Yet, she is now worried about her remaining academic subjects during the second semester and fears her pregnancy is going to interfere. During the last week of the end of semester exam fortnight she is in panic mode. Exams are in full swing but she only has two exams. One of her lecturers takes her aside and quietly tells her that she doesn't look well. She asks if there is anything Cathy would like to tell her. An experienced mature woman, she can see the signs of late pregnancy. She is looking exhausted. Her eyes have dark shadows, she has back pain, and has to make frequent trips to the toilet. Cathy graciously accepts her caring concern. Yet, she will not talk but assures her everything is okay. The lecturer feels she doesn't want to or shouldn't interfere.

Cathy is tired and very worried about her family's reaction to her pregnancy. So, she is procrastinating. After the exam fortnight she lingers at University and in her unit. She spends a whole day meticulously tidying up her little unit. Finally, on Thursday 15 November she decides to drive home. It's only just over a four hour journey but she is getting desperate. End of pregnancy hormones are making her scatty like this. Maybe her parents will help her, now. She needs her family. She'll confess all to them. They'll have contacts to help. How they can help, she doesn't know. She packs a small suitcase of clothes, some books and her toiletries bag.

Just before leaving Toowoomba, she calls in at the Coles supermarket in the shopping mall opposite her block of units and spends over $90 to buy a rather random selection of non-perishable grocery items to give to her parents. They include things like Weet-Bix, jam, peanut butter, sugar, soap powder, dishwashing liquid, sultanas, two rolls of paper towels, toilet paper, instant coffee, tea bags and several other items, including a packet of Tim Tams[32] which her father loves.

She leaves town shortly before 3:30 p.m. on that Thursday afternoon hoping to get home by about eight in the evening and surprise her parents. It's a four and a half hour journey.

Just as she reaches Wallangarra on the border with NSW and about 180km south of Toowoomba, she feels a bit dizzy. It is around 6:15 p.m. She has made good time. She pulls over on the roadside at Jennings, less than 50 metres across the border. That is when she feels a slight contracting urge in her lower abdomen. She realises it could be a first contraction. "Oh, dearie me. I have to get home! God, please help me."

The contraction passes.

She prays.

She drives on.

On entering Tenterfield 20km later, there is a second small contraction like that previous one. She pulls over, takes deep breaths and counts. In two minutes, it is over. She prays again.

Driving into the town, she sees the signpost for the Tenterfield District Hospital. She turns off the main street and into Naas Street and up the hill to the Hospital and into Pelham Street. She parks at the Emergency section. She is supposed to press a button and talk to somebody inside. This is the after hours system.

The rear of Tenterfield Hospital. When Cathy arrived and tried go to the Emergency section on the left, it was getting dark.

---

[32] Tim Tams are a very popular chocolate coated biscuit.

Put off by this, she turns the car around. She heads south.

She has another small contraction at Bluff Rock and pulls over at the rest area there. She breathes heavily and counts. Then, it's over in two minutes. The evening air is getting cooler.

She drives on. There is another little contraction at Sandy Flat, just eight minutes after the last one. She does the same thing, breathes heavily and counts. She drives on. Another contraction at the top of Bolivia Hill. This time it is 15 minutes after the last one. She does the same again.

It's almost dark, now. It's November and the summer sun sets later. And, with calm still conditions, a clear sky, and the higher altitude, the night is promising to be quite cool.

Going down the southern slope of Bolivia Hill, there is another contraction starting to come on. It is now 8:30 p.m. and well over an hour since the first contraction at Jennings. But, it is only five minutes after the end of the last one. This time, she feels it's a big one. After feeling the contraction just beginning, it suddenly becomes intense and very painful. The urge to push is uncontrollable, very strong, and continuous. It's as if she has an urgent, urgent need to poo. But, there is nowhere to pull over and stop. She is really desperate. She wants to stop in the middle of the road and just get out. Then, she sees and pulls into a little track at the side of the road. It is not easy to notice speeding past along the highway. But, in her sense of urgency, she spots it. She brakes suddenly and hard. She reverses back to it and turns into it. She is desperate and just needs somewhere to pull over. It's not an official rest area. The short 40 metre track opens out into a large clearing where Main Roads Department workers can leave road construction gravel or aggregate, crushed blue metal, and other road making equipment. Even though it is now dark, the trees, grass, and piles of crushed metal and gravel are easily seen with her car's headlights.

As seen in daylight, the NSW Main Roads Department stockpile site ST50079 turn off is on the left. At night it harder to see.

As soon as she stops near some grass at the side of the clearing, she slips the car into 'Park', switches off the motor but not the headlights.

There is intense lower back pain.

With a cloudless black sky, the night air is cool at 1000 metres. She's still wearing that long dress. But, she just has to get out of the car. She is driven to get out. It's so very urgent!

In desperate panic, she pushes the door open with great force. It almost bounces back on her. Her seatbelt hasn't even retracted fully as she jumps out and tries to stand up but finds herself automatically parting her legs and bending her knees. Her body has taken over. The uncontrolled pushing down is so strong. It is totally involuntary.

Then whooosh!

Her waters have broken. Her pants are soaked and amniotic fluid rushes down her legs. It's on her dress, too.

She realises that the baby's head is now pushing into her pants. It's coming and fast!

She is able to quickly remove one leg from her pants, holding on to the car door as she does so. She tries to squat on the ground but she cries out with the really strong pain as a massive muscular spasm takes over.

She falls over onto her back.

There is gigantic push.

It's coming out!

She howls.

Then, there is the baby lying on the ground and between her legs partially on the long skirt she is wearing. The umbilical cord is still connected to the placenta which remains inside her.[33]

She relaxes.

The time is around 9:00 p.m. and only around one and a half hours since that first very mild contraction at Jennings on the Queensland/NSW border.

---

[33] For a graphic example of this kind rushed birth: https://www.documentingreality.com/forum/f225/woman-gives-birth-outside-mexican-clinic-after-being-denied-medical-attention-134585/ and https://www.medicaldaily.com/irma-lopez-aurelio-gives-birth-outside-mexican-clinic-after-being-denied-immediate-medical-attention These reports and the publication of the dramatic photo are by Irma Lopez, a professor of Spanish and an anthropologist at Western Michigan University at Kalamazoo in the USA.

She relaxes to catch her breath.

The car's door courtesy light and some glow from the headlights give her some illumination.

She sits up and looks at this baby. It's a tiny baby.

She thinks: 'No wonder it came out so quickly. … And, it's covered in amniotic fluid, blood and vernix. Looks so mucky, just like a new-born lamb. … No, looks worse! Lambs are cute.'

Still sitting on the ground and less than five minutes later, there is another easier contraction and out comes the placenta with another quick whoosh!

She breathes another sigh, a heavy sigh of relief.

Now, she can hear the calm silence of the bush.

Shock sets in. "What has happened?!! What am I doing here?"

The baby starts crying, a typical tremulous newborn cry but it is not very loud. So, she realises that it is alive.

She sits up and looks at this "parasite" which has finally come out of her. Oh, the relief! In the glow from the car's lights, she can see its face is all crumpled and wrinkly. It looks horrible. So ugly. Face all screwed up. She can see clearly that it's a girl. And, that vernix all over it. What a mess! She has no sympathy with it or its sudden but weak and appealing crying. She is feeling considerable pain in her abdomen.

The baby, with the placenta next to it, is lying partly on the hard gravel ground and partly on her long skirt.[34]

Sitting on the hard gravel, she leans back against the car.

---

[34] This kind of birth is not too uncommon. A simple *Google* search of 'Woman gives birth standing' will reveal many cases with photos and video clips of these events. For a typical example in the Singapore newspaper *The Straits Times* about a birth in the street in China. At first, bystanders just stand and stare while some stand and film the action. When the baby is finally on the ground, some help the mother. Afterwards, the woman can be seen calmly walking home with her new baby: https://stomp.straitstimes.com/singapore-seen/chinese-woman-gives-birth-to-baby-while-standing-on- street-then-walks-home-as-if-it
   A rapid birth is termed "precipitous labour" and usually occurs after less than three hours of labour. Most cases of precipitous labour occur with "multiparous" women (who have had several births) but in around 10% of cases the mothers are "nulliparous" (no previous births). Complications can result from a very rapid delivery but in this Japanese study it was found that "precipitous labor seemed to be not associated with adverse maternal outcomes". Complications were usually associated with other factors. A likely contributor to precipitous labour in teenage deliveries is a pre-term birth, a soft birth canal, and a small foetus. Suzuki, S. (2015), "Clinical Significance of Precipitous Labor". *Journal of Clinical Medicine Research*, March 2015, 7(3), pages 150-153. https://www.ncbi.nlm.nih.gov/pmc/articles/ PMC4285060/

She howls in pain.

"Oh, dear God! This is awful! … Arrrgh … Arrrrrrrgh! Oh, dear God! Please help me! … Please! … Please!"

She goes quiet apart from steady whimpering.

The baby is still crying weakly.

Finally, Cathy stands up. As she does so, the baby and placenta are tipped off her long dress skirt and onto the ground. Although standing at the side of the car, she can see the baby clearly in the spread out diffused glow from the headlights.

Yes, it is a small baby. Even in her condition and state of trauma, she can see that. It crosses her mind that it might not even survive. Small lambs often don't.

She leans against the car again and continues whimpering.

She removes her other leg from her underpants and leaves them on the ground.

The pain in her lower abdomen is intense, like a really big stitch she sometimes gets while jogging. This lasts for up to ten minutes. Then, it gradually slows in intensity.

The baby is still crying but not strongly. It is the only sound in the otherwise totally silent bush night.

Cathy: "Oh, shut up! Please shut up! … Please! … Please!"

She is really, really distraught, stressed, and in pain.

She staggers around to the back to the car, opens the rear hatch or boot and takes out a roll of kitchen paper towels from one of the two Coles re-usable plastic shopping bags she has the gift groceries for her parents in. She opens the paper towel pack and grabs some. She hitches up her long skirt and starts wiping herself down, in her crotch and up and down both her legs. Her long dress is very mucky with amniotic fluid and blood.

Not quite knowing how to handle this yukkie human baby, she tips the contents of one of the Coles plastic bags into the boot or hatch at the back of he car. Among those groceries is that opened pack of paper towels. She grabs wads of paper towels and carrying the now empty Coles plastic bag steps back to the baby on the ground, picks up her messy underpants and puts them into the plastic bag. She wipes herself more with paper towels and tips them into the plastic bag. Then, holding paper towels in her hands, she gingerly picks up the baby and placenta together and places them into the plastic bag. The placenta falls in first.

She thinks to herself: "I'll toss it into the bush."

Although the car's engine is not running, the headlights are still on.

In the glow of the car's headlights, she carries the bag and its contents to a small clump of grass around 50 metres away from the entrance of the clearing. She leaves the bag on the ground.

She returns to her car. She stands next to the driver's door and wipes herself at the crotch some more. The is some more blood. Then, going to the rear hatch, she opens her suitcase and takes out a towel, folds it in half and places it on the driver's seat.

She takes another long dress out of her suitcase and changes into this clean dress. She wipes her crotch more. She puts on some clean underpants. She empties another grocery bag and puts her dirty dress into it. 'I'll wash it at home.' She leaves that plastic bag in the car's boot or hatch. She closes up the suitcase and the rear hatch. She gets into the driver's seat and sits there thinking for a moment. But, she doesn't close the door.

She is in lingering pain.

She hears the baby's crying. It's not strong.

She wonders. "What have I done! Oh God! That baby is all alone."

Guilt and caring emotions come to the fore.

"I'll go and fetch her back."

She gets out of the car again but stands still.

The crying has stopped. She wonders: "Is it dead?"

She says to herself: "Well, I didn't make that baby. It was put inside me by a bunch of misogynous rats! And, I don't even know who they were! It's not mine! I don't want it. I hate it! It's a parasite! And, my body has ejected it. It's dead! It's gone!"

But then, the baby's crying starts up again.

She looks over to where the baby is. In the glow from her car's lights, she can see the bag. Should she go and fetch it? If she does, what can she do with it? What will her parents say? Especially, how will her mother react? "She'll be ropable. No, I couldn't face her. Anyway, it's a parasite and I don't want it."

Standing outside the car, hearing the crying is worrying her. She is vacilating over what to do with this baby, the baby which has caused her so much grief. Her conservative Anglican Christianity which she has always seen as a guiding light for how to conduct her life with kindness and social justice is now being thoroughly tested. Sorely troubled by her situation, she cries out: "Oh, God. Please help me, please, please. What did I do to deserve this? God, please guide me!"

Standing next to the car, she repeatedly looks towards the crying baby around 10 metres away from her at the edge of the clearing.

The baby is still crying quietly over near the grass. It's not strong or loud crying but it's still the distressed, quivering, and imploring crying of a helpless baby desperate for compassion. It's a classic newborn cry that tugs on the heartstrings of most adults.

Confused, tormented, and still in pain, she reacts more negatively to the crying: "Oh, shut up! Go away! I can't stand your crying. You're not mine! Go away! … Just shut up will you! … Just die, can't you!"

Saying "shut up" is most unusual for Cathy with her prim and proper upbringing. But, she is extremely upset, alone, and going through a major bout of perinatal depression.[35] Moreover, while going through this trauma, she is all alone and isolated in the bush in the middle of the night. Not a good scenario for a birth! Thus, she makes a capricious decision. [36]

---

[35]   "What is perinatal depression?" *American Psychiatric Association*. (2024), https://www.psychiatry.org/patients-families/peripartum-depression/what-is-peripartum-depression

[36]   Not all mothers of babies conceived through rape hate their babies. Many don't but here is a classic case of one who does: "10 months on, the babies of Rohingya rape survivors arrive". *RNS Religious News Service*, 29 May 2019. Columbia, USA. https://religionnews.com/2018/07/05/10-months-on-the-babies-of-rohingya-rape-survivors-arrive/ During the Rwandan genocide of April to July 1994, an estimated 800,000 people were killed. Up to 500,000 women and girls were raped, giving birth to between 10,000 and 25,000 "children of bad memories" or *les enfants de mauvais souvenir*. Mitchell, K. 2005. "Children born from rape: Overlooked victims of human rights violations in conflict settings". *Paper presented in Master of Public Health Capstone Symposium*, May 14, 2005, Johns Hopkins Bloomberg School of Public Health Baltimore, Maryland.

One survivor, Jacqueline, was gang-raped and became pregnant with her daughter Angel as a result. Although she was initially so traumatised by the assault that she tried to poison herself and her baby daughter, she eventually entered counselling and "started to love her" and now feels her baby called Angel came from God. Paquette, D., "Turning pain into hope". *Washington Post*, 11 June 2017. https://www.washingtonpost.com/sf/world/2017/06/11/rwandas-children- of-rape-are-coming-of-age-against-the-odds/?utm_term=.2087559cc31c

Yet, there are still mothers who give birth and hate the infant they have just brought into this world: Roughley, L., "Remorseless mum who stabbed newborn baby to death with scissors jailed for life". *Daily Mirror*, London, 06 February 2019. https://www.mirror.co.uk/news/uk-news/remorseless-mum-who-stabbed-newborn-13961897?utm_source=mirror_newsletter&utm_medium=email&utm_content=EM_Mirror_Nletter_DailyNews_News_smalltease r_Image_Story&utm_campaign=daily_newsletter This mature woman with a postgraduate degree in forensic psychology gave birth alone to a baby she did not want.

All this has been happening so quickly.

She grits her teeth angrily, gets back into the car, slams the door, starts the engine, puts it into 'Drive', and, with the front wheels spinning on the loose gravel, does a u-turn, and heads out to the highway.[37] She turns left and heads south. She has decided to go straight home and doesn't want to get home too late for her parents as it is after 9:30 p.m. So, she's driving fast.

She drives straight through Deepwater. And, she drives through Glen Innes. She should have checked in at a motel but she is not thinking straight. Still in pain, feeling bouts of weakness, and anxious, she is distraught and frenzied. When an approaching car doesn't dip its headlights she is ropable. But, eventually she swings to a more tolerant compassionate mood. She is not quite with it. She thinks of the baby she left behind at Bolivia Hill. She swings back into anger.

About 90 minutes later, it is 11:00 p.m. At the turn off to Tubbamurra Road to go to the family property at Hampden Downs, she pulls over. She is very worried and deep in thought: 'Oh, I feel terrible. I left a tiny little baby all alone in the bush. … She was crying for me. … I just left her, alone in the dark. How could I do that?! I wouldn't do that to a newborn lamb. … She's a newborn human baby who came out of me! How could you! … Oh, God, please help me. … I can't leave her. I just can't. … Okay, I'll go back to her. I'll take her home. Mother and Dad will just have to wear it. … Yes, I'll go back to her.'

So, she decides to drive back to the baby.

But, while still in her postpartum shock and depression, she makes a disastrous mistake.

Before doing a U-turn, she waits for an oncoming car to pass. In her anguished state of mind and in the dark, her judgement is impaired. She does not look behind

---

[37] Another recent case where a young girl does not want the baby she has just given birth to: she is an 18-year-old American from a well-off family who was on a high school graduate students 'gap year' group tour of Europe. After giving birth in her Paris hotel room, she wrapped the baby in a sheet and threw it out of the window down to the street 10 metres below. The baby did not survive. Fagge, N., "American student, 18, who hurled her newborn baby from Paris hotel room to its death". *Daily Mail*, London, 27 February 2025. https://www.dailymail.co.uk/news/ article-14435665/Mia-McQuillin-Oregon-identified-baby-Paris-hurled-death.html?
More on this tragedy: "US Mother Who Dropped Baby To Death In Paris Placed In Psychiatric Care." *NDTV* https://www.ndtv.com/world-news/us-mother-who-dropped-baby-to-death-in-paris-placed-in-psychiatric-care-7807258
And: "Elle jette son nourrisson depuis la fenêtre d'un hôtel." *Paris Match*, 24 Feb 2025. https://www.parismatch.com/ actu/faits-divers/info-paris-match-paris-elle-jette-son-nourrisson-depuis-la-fenetre-dun-hotel-247815

and check her mirror. As soon as that car passes, impulsively and not appreciating that there is another set of headlights coming up fast from behind her, she pulls out and does a U-turn right into the path of a B-Double truck coming down hill at nearly 100km/h.

This is the scene of the accident as seen in daylight. The truck driver had little chance to avoid hitting Cathy's Kia Cerato hard. The turnoff to the Hampton Downs farm is on the left.

A terrible, terrible mistake.

She didn't even turn her indicator lights on to signal what she was doing.

The driver hits the horn and desperately brakes. He shouts to himself: "Bloody hell!!!"

Even though it is a modern Scania truck with ABS brakes, it is too late.

The big truck hits Cathy's car hard on the driver's side.

BANG!!! WHAM!!!

Her car is pushed to the other side of the highway. Cathy is trapped in the crumpled wreck.

The truck driver pulls up as fast as he can. With a solid bull-bar at the front, it suffers only minor or cosmetic damage. He gets out and runs to help.

A typical B-Double truck with a robust bull-bar. (*Scania photo*)

Unfortunately, the front of Cathy's car now bursts into flames.

The truck driver and some other motorists rush to get Cathy out. They can't open the driver's door. They get the front passenger door open. Despite the heat and flames, the truck driver leans inside from the passenger side. He struggles to get her seat belt undone. Finally, just in time he manages to do so. He drags her out across the passenger seat.

The truck driver and other motorists lie her on the ground well clear of the burning car. They put out flames on her dress and in doing so they have to remove much of the dress. They try to comfort her. They can see she is badly burned and both legs are obviously broken.

Of course, another motorist has used their mobile phone to call 000. So, help is on the way.

On the ground now, Cathy is conscious, in shock, and in pain. She cries out: "Oh God, please forgive me! Please help that baby! … Help her, please! … I'm so sorry! … Please!"

To her helpers, she is delirious. They have no idea what she is on about.

Surprisingly soon, an ambulance and a fire engine arrive from Guyra just 15km to the south.

Soon after Cathy has been dragged out of the burning car by the truck driver, firefighters from Guyra arrived to put out the fire. Everything inside Cathy's Kia Cerato was burned and the car ended up a gutted charred hulk. And, Cathy is terribly injured and burned. (*BP News* photo)

The ambulance crew see her broken legs and burns. They also notice bleeding at her groin and her distorted and crushed pelvis.[38] They assume there is internal bleeding.

Yet, despite her horrific injuries, Cathy is feeling a kind of resurrection. She's suddenly happy and relieved that it is all over. She is thinking of that baby. She is now convinced it will be okay. Guilt has left her. It has evaporated. She is thinking of a painting she liked by Finnish artist Akseli Gallen-Kallela. It looks rather like her. She smiles. She is reassured. She's in a semi-delirious dream world. She talks aloud: "Thank you, God. Thank you, thank you. Help for that little one has arrived. She'll be safe and cared for. … I can let go now. Thank you so much. Amen."

Adastra - the resurrection.
Akseli Gallen-Kallela, 1907
(*Public domain*.)

---

38 See: "Pelvic fracture", *Wikipedia*. https://en.wikipedia.org/wiki/Pelvic_fracture Complications may include internal bleeding, injury to the bladder and vaginal trauma. These are all features of Cathy's injuries.

Paramedics don't have a clue what she is on about and ignore it. They are focussed on their patient's physical welfare. In the ambulance they sedate her using a drip. She loses consciousness.

The ambulance heads down the hill towards Guyra with lights and siren blazing.

Then, Cathy's breathing slows and her pulse weakens. Worried, the paramedics work desperately to save her. They fear cardiac arrest. They get the driver to pull over. They place two patches from the on-board defibrillator onto her chest. A paramedic presses the 'Analyse' key, hoping it will tell them something. At that very moment her heart starts fibrillating.[39] Her body is shutting down. Her heart is going into cardiac arrest.[40] The defibrillator immediately flashes **DELIVER SHOCK**. The paramedic quickly selects 'Manual' and she sets the energy level for her patient's estimated age and weight. It whines as it charges up. She shouts "All clear!" The team moves back as she holds down the key with the 'heart' symbol on it. Cathy is given an electric shock. Her frame lurches up for a second or so. Then, it relaxes down.

The crew breathes a collective sigh of relief as her heart reverts to a more stable rhythm. Cathy is given intravenous blood replacement fluids, and coma-inducing drugs. The ambulance crew watch her closely for the last few kilometres into Guyra. On entry to Guyra she is in cardiac arrest again. The ambulance stops at the roadside. Pressed for time, they desperately try simple CPR[41] for nearly ten minutes but to no avail. She dies in the ambulance.

At the Guyra Hospital and later, nobody discovered that she had recently given birth. Her smashed pelvis, injured abdomen and bleeding at her groin masked that. That injury and the severe burns dominated the autopsy. The ambulance paramedics were interviewed and completed a report for the coroner. Thus, the

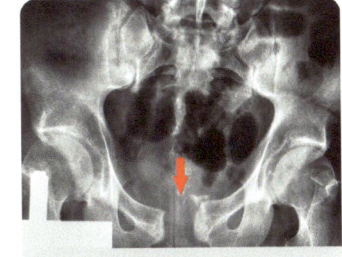

(Broken pelvis. *Wikipedia*.)

---

39 Ventricular fibrillation: an uncoordinated weak heart beat which does not circulate blood, ends blood supply to the brain and death results. The defibrillator is used to shock the heart into a more regular beat. https://en.wikipedia.org/ wiki/Fibrillation. [The example used here of a defibrillator is the 'Corpuls3' when it is switched to 'manual' mode.]

40 "What is cardiac arrest?" https://www.heartfoundation.org.au/bundles/your-heart/cardiac-arrest

41 See: "Cardiopulmonary resuscitation", *Wikipedia*: https://en.wikipedia.org/wiki/Cardiopulmonary_resuscitation

eventual coroner's report was brief and focussed on the burns, broken pelvis, resulting internal injury and bleeding, and of course her deteriorating coronary function. All these were put down to the horrific accident. They even X-rayed her broken pelvis. Nobody even considered a birth.

Ironically, about thirty minutes before this horrific accident happened, Keith was heading north and driving home past the Tubbamurra turnoff. Later his VW campervan and Cathy's Kia Cerato passed each other just ten kilometres south of Glen Innes as she headed south and he was driving north. Then, as she was being stretchered into the ambulance at the Tubbamurra turnoff and she was calling out to God thanking him for saving the baby, that was the very moment Keith decided to stop and drive into that Bolivia Hill clearing at the same Stockpile site ST50079. He was tired and feeling sleepy. Sensibly, he didn't want to fall asleep at the wheel. So, he would bed down for the night in his campervan.

As we know, he was in for a shock after he woke up at sunrise and quite casually checked his surroundings.

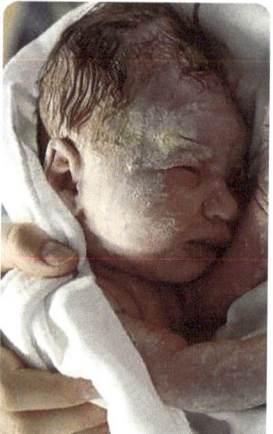

(Left) This is what Keith saw on his arrival at Bolivia Hill late at night. But, he was tired and didn't investigate the Coles plastic bag until the morning. (Right) In the morning, he found the baby still alive. (Dreamstime photo. Model)

Next day Cathy's body is taken to the morgue at Armidale.

Her parents are deeply shocked.

A week later, there is a short small funeral for her at the St James Anglican Church in Guyra. But, there are many more mourners than expected. Cathy was well known in pony club and riding circles as well as among regular parishioners. It is a very sad and traditional service with that classic hymn "Abide with me …"[42] causing a massive outpouring of grief in the Church.

St James Anglican Church at Guyra.

Cathy's mother and father are profoundly upset. Her mother is now feeling very guilty about all those seventeen years of parenting her daughter in a strict and cold way. Her father realises this and comforts her. They are also particularly saddened that, now in their late seventies, they have lost their only child.

About two weeks after Cathy's funeral, her mother and father drive to Toowoomba to check on her unit and arrange for its sale. Her mother is increasingly suffering from dementia and finds it all too much.

Cathy's father finds her diary in her unit in Toowoomba. For some reason she didn't take it with her. Perhaps, she was cautious about privacy. Anyway, it is not a diary filled with personal detail. More often, it records when letters were posted and received, bills were paid, when assignments were due and submitted, and when her car was serviced. Though, there are very occasionally quite short personal entries, for example, she mentions when she was attacked while out jogging. She used a now favourite word of hers: 'Kicked the misogynist in the face. He ran.'

She mentions attending Dale Spender's lecture: 'Loved it! Joined Women's Network.'

She records each of the many times she attended meetings of the Toowoomba University Women's Network. She even mentions in late October when she was elected to the committee as a first year student rep. Nevertheless, it seems from her diary that she didn't attend Women's Network social functions but mentions that she had long conversations with fourth year Law student Elizabeth Melrose. These were a month before her fateful drive home on 15 November.

---

[42] For an excellent rendition by the Choir of Kings College, Cambridge: https://www.youtube.com/watch?v=PmjuqZSH_aY (Reach for the box of tissues.)

However, an early entry for Sunday 18 March stands out. Cathy's diary just says 'Drink spiked and raped. Who?'

Then the entry for Monday 19th March 2018 briefly says: 'Kind Elizabeth of Woman's Network told me it may have not been just one man but could have been a gang rape. Evil young men drugged me and raped me on Saturday night. Deeply shocked at what they did to me. Yeurrrk! Can't tell a soul. Ashamed.'

The only other reference to the rape is for Wednesday 14 November: 'Think I'll drive home tomorrow and confess all to Mother and Father. Mother will be furious. Hope Father will be more kind. Maybe they can help. God, please help me. I'll leave for home tomorrow afternoon. Must take some groceries for Mother.'

That is the last entry in her diary.

There was no reference to her pregnancy anywhere in the diary.

After three weeks, Cathy's father shows the diary to the Police in Armidale. For them, the main thing it reveals is that she was raped, likely a gang rape, and when it happened following a drink spiking. But, they note that it was not reported. They also note that there is no mention of any boyfriend in the diary. It is clear that after the rape and, with her joining the Women's Network, she had become very negative about males. They track down Elizabeth Melrose of the Women's Network. She confirms Cathy's rape trauma but she is genuinely unable to give any names of suspected perpetrators. However, as a newly qualified lawyer and knowing about the pregnancy, out of respect for Cathy she cautiously says nothing about it. Police don't even consider it.

Toying with the notion that the rapists had already left the University and aware that trying to track down ex-students can be difficult, especially when they don't have any names, the Police investigation loses momentum. After many months the Police investigation slows right down. Within a year it has become inactive, goes cold, and is filed as such.

Cathy's death had a little mention in the local *Northern Tablelands Examiner*. The paper made a small one paragraph mention on page 3 about the death of a 17-year-old girl after a horrendous accident at the Tubbamurra turn-off. They did mention her name, Catherine Morton, and said she was well-known and much respected in the community. Despite the sizeable attendance at her funeral, the community moves on.

Meanwhile, her gang rapists have no idea of what has happened and the truly awful consequences of their short few minutes of toxic male sexual gratification last March. The three gang rapists have graduated with three-year Commerce degrees and have left the University. They soon found jobs far away in Sydney. And, with all three working in the central business district, they stay in contact. None of them knows Cathy is dead or that she died traumatised after giving birth to a baby one of them is father of.

When they meet for occasional lunchtime pub reunions, Cathy is just one of the girls those misogynistic young men have a giggle about over a few beers. As with the rapists in Ingham during the 1970s, they also believe that girls exist solely for the sexual pleasure of men: a notion still common today as seen in the success of on-line influencers like Andrew Tate. His influence even extends to very young boys like two 11-year-old boys in foster care who strangled and sexually abused girls also in care.[43] And, toxic masculinity occurs among even very little boys.[44] But, as we've seen with what went on in Ingham, sex attacks on girls are not new.

---

[43] Fellows, T. "Girl strangled in care." *Courier Mail*, Brisbane, 12 July 2023, page 3. https://www.couriermail. com.au/subscribe/news/1/?qld-juvie-home-crisis-girl-allegedly-strangled-assaulted-by-11yo-boy (There is a paywall on this story.) Girls were strangled Andrew Tate style. A grandmother complained about the sexual assaults of girls in foster care by two 11-year-old boys but the Department of Child Safety did nothing. 'She was strangled by another boy.' When the girl complained, the carer 'didn't want the matter going any further.' The excuse was 'I believe it has not been properly documented'. However, 'it only got reported when the girl attended school the next day and told her teacher'. This is typical of attempts to sweep these allegations under the carpet because they are too damaging to foster carers and the Department.

[44] Classic toxic masculinity is something which is sometimes rife among school boys especially teenagers. Is it on the rise? This author doubts it. It is not new. The author can remember this culture of boys tormenting school girls in a sexual way from his primary school years in the 1950s.

Yet, today toxic masculinity exists even with very little boys like these five-year-olds who gang raped or 'sexually assaulted' a five-year-old girl: Huang, D. "Sydney school rattled as five-year-old girl allegedly 'sexually assaulted' on playground by a group of boys." *7 News*, Sydney, 31 March 2025. https://7news.com. au/news/sydney-school-rattled-as- five-year-old-girl-allegedly-sexually-assaulted-on-playground-by-a-group-of-boys-c-18217375 Yes, the boys were only five-years-old! The girl was seriously injured internally and needed hospital treatment to enable her to urinate.

Achenza, M. "Australian teachers expose disturbing trend of toxic masculinity in schools", *ABC News*, Sydney 04 April 2024. https://www.news.com.au/lifestyle/parenting/school-life/australian-teachers-expose-disturbing-trend-of-toxic-masculinity-in-schools/news-story/e258e309559c2f971c8ea70a1f93b169

Wescott, S. & Roberts, S. "Research exposes alarming impact of 'manfluencer' culture on Australian schools." 03 April 2024, Monash University, Melbourne. https://www.monash.edu/news/articles/research-exposes-alarming-impact-of-manfluencer-culture-on-australian-schools

Sadly, Eppie and Keith never find out why she was abandoned at Bolivia Hill. They never find out who her birth mother was or what had happened to her. They never found out how like Eppie she was and the good person she was. But, because of what Keith did for and with a baby he found abandoned at Bolivia Hill, in so many ways Cathy now lives on in her daughter. And, Eppie has inherited her biological mother's misandry.

After an 18-year-old man beat, strangled, and attempted to rape her Andrew Tate style while she was in foster care, six-year-old Eppie discussed with Keith her feelings of hatred for men and boys. Yet, he is the man she adores. Astute and introspective little Eppie understood the contradiction in what she said to him: "Mumma, I still really hate men and boys. They give me the shits. I can't change that. It's in me. Maybe that lady who gave birth to me at Bolivia Hill had big problems with men. Yes, that could be it. And, it's been passed on to me. … Then you came along at Bolivia Hill and straight away started giving me real care and love. But, you're not a woman. That's upset things."[45]

17-year-old Cathy the morning before giving birth to Eppie that evening and her death 2 hours later. (*Dreamstime*. Model.)

6-year-old Eppie six years after Cathy's death. (*iStockphoto*. Model.)

79-year-old Keith six years after finding newborn Eppie. (*Glenphoto*. Model.)

---

[45] See: Sapolsky, R. (2023), *Determined: Life without Free Will*. The Bodley Head (Penguin), London. Sapolsky says our behaviour has genetic underpinnings inherited from our parents' lives and shaped probably even at our conception. Thus, Cathy's pregnancy was a formative time for Eppie's misandry.

www.ingramcontent.com/pod-product-compliance
Lightning Source LLC
Chambersburg PA
CBHW041429120626
46547CB00002B/151